ANNE STEVENSON-YANG, originally from Washington, DC, was a journalist in New York when she moved to Beijing in 1993 with the US–China Business Council. In over a quarter of a century living in China, she founded companies in publishing, software and online media. Today, back in the US, she runs J Capital Research USA and is the author of *China Alone: China's Emergence and Potential Return to Isolation*.

First published in the United Kingdom by Bui Jones 2024
Copyright © Anne Stevenson-Yang

Anne Stevenson-Yang has asserted her right under the Copyright,
Designs and Patents Act 1988 to be identified as the author of this work

BUI JONES

buijones.com
Bui Jones Limited Company Number 14823240

Printed and bound in Great Britain by Clays Ltd, Elcograf S.p.A.
A CIP catalogue record for this book is available from the British Library
ISBN 978-1-7394243-1-2

MIX
Paper | Supporting
responsible forestry
FSC
www.fsc.org
FSC® C018072

All Bui Jones books are printed on
paper from responsible sources.

WILD RIDE

A short history of the opening and closing
of the Chinese economy

Anne Stevenson-Yang

BUI JONES

For S & L, who are shockingly supportive of me.

CONTENTS

PREFACE

In 1985, I was invited to work as a "foreign expert" in Beijing for the magazine *China Pictorial*, published by the Foreign Languages Press under China's Ministry of Culture. *China Pictorial* was a government-owned propaganda publication distributed through embassies overseas. It stretched to 24 pages a month, consisting of grainy pictures with paragraph-long captions about China's happy national minorities and agricultural achievements. The magazine had about 300 employees. I had previously worked at *Business Week* in New York, which ran to about 64 pages each week and, though famously overstaffed, had about a third as many employees.

The 300 staffers at *China Pictorial* were distributed through 18 language sections, including Indonesian, even though the

Indonesian edition had not been published since China broke off relations with Indonesia after the 1965 coup attempt, which President Suharto accused China of supporting. The Indonesian section still employed five translators. One of them fixed radios for everyone else and took a lot of naps on the cot he had installed in the office. Another wrote poetry. And another would spend the days walking up and down the halls kicking the skirting boards and muttering.

Employees received basic healthcare at the office clinic, where a huge whiteboard kept track publicly of how many condoms each employee had taken in a given month. All the young and unmarried staff lived in the office, generally sleeping on top of desks, because there was a shortage of housing available to them from *China Pictorial*. Those who had been lucky enough to be allocated an apartment (that usually happened a few years after getting married or after turning 40) had small cold-water flats owned and managed by the magazine in a nearby compound.

There was little to do each day, but people were required to turn up, so they played ping pong, chain-smoked (Chinese people at the time universally believed that smoking protected the lungs), played cards, and snoozed in the office. Several people applied repeatedly to be permitted to leave and find another job, but permission was never granted, since the magazine received government subsidies based partly on headcount, and because there were no other jobs, and no one wanted to be responsible for unemployment. Staff received pay each month in cash. The ¥10 note was the largest then printed, and the average editor, photographer, or translator got six tens, now the equivalent of less than US$10, per month. Pay went towards extras, like cigarettes; housing, food, and utilities were provided almost for free.

I learned at *China Pictorial* how stultifying and unproductive the system was, even when it was taking care of people's most basic needs. Employees were treated like children, restricted as to where they could go and what they could do. Marriage or travel required written permission from the office leader. Work was pointless, and no one had incentive to do more than the bare minimum, if that. Everyone had to spend Saturdays in "political study" discussing in what way their thoughts might not support the Communist Party. Food was so basic that a major topic of conversation was where some delicacy, sweet potatoes or fish, for example, could be bought. The government delivered stacks of Napa cabbages to each home at the start of winter, and people would peel off a few leaves to stir-fry and eat with rice each evening, leaving the rest outside to stay naturally chilled – few families had refrigerators, and those who did proudly displayed them in their living rooms, adorned with a doily. Cultural activities consisted of viewing patriotic films using tickets handed out at the office or exercising in the park. Lucky people with good connections might be able to see an acrobatics show once a year.

About a month into my tenure at the magazine, an office mate told me his father had died of tuberculosis.

"But that's normally curable," I said. "Didn't the doctor diagnose it correctly?"

The colleague laughed. "We are farmers; we don't have money to see doctors." With one sentence, my belief in Maoism as the system that made people's lives better was thrown into doubt. It was my first realisation that "socialism" in China was reserved for the urban privileged.

*

I lingered in China, first to learn the language, then because I married there. In 1988, I told the Hindi translator I'd married that I needed to go back to the US to recharge. I was mentally exhausted by trying to fit in. At the time, we had only one day off a week. I would look forward to sleeping in, but around 7:30 a.m. each Sunday, my new in-laws would appear at the front gate (no one had telephones back then) ready to stay all day, cooking, napping, taking baths in my hot-water apartment, and watching TV. I was obliged to speak Chinese constantly, which made me feel stupid, as my vocabulary was very limited. I could never get titles right. In China, when you arrive at a gathering, you need to say the title of each person you encounter in rank order, and the titles are excruciatingly specific – maternal mother-in-law, older brother-in-law, older brother-in-law's wife, and so on down the line. I could never remember all the titles and would be tongue-tied for fear I might mix up words like *bomu* (a respectful title for an older woman) with *baomu* (housemaid). So we moved to Washington to rejoin what I viewed as the real world.

Then, in 1993, an investment association called the US-China Business Council invited me to head their China operations in Beijing. At the time, there were few Americans available who knew anything about China, so they were willing to hire a journalist-cum-magazine-editor for much more money than I had ever earned. The Council, as we called it, had been a fairly sleepy DC association dedicated to improving US-China ties, but during my time there – 1993 to 1998 – foreign investment in China was exploding. Having grown up in Washington, DC, I knew nothing about business. When the head of Ford automobiles came to visit, I mistakenly pulled the file on FMC (a chemicals company, which I mistook for Ford Motor Company). I had a vague idea that GE made light bulbs and Exxon (or Esso?) sold gasoline. No matter: staffers for CEOs coming through Beijing had to plug holes in the executives' schedules, so they generally added 'a visit to Anne at the Council'. I would sit there listening to CEOs talk about their business units' struggles to enter the market. They told me far more than they would have told a journalist, and it was a fascinating glimpse into the mechanics of the economy.

A few months in, I figured it would be good for me to see the provinces, and I took a business trip to a trade fair in the ancient capital nestled in the centre of the country, Xi'an, where 2,000 years ago, the first Qin emperor built his magnificent tomb, guarded by an army of terracotta warriors. On my first morning in Xi'an, I walked the short distance from hotel to exhibition centre to attend the conference being held before the fair. Two ladies wearing red sashes ushered me through a door and up some stairs. I thought it odd to enter this way – maybe I was late and everyone else was seated – but I was excited to hear whoever was going to speak, and I pressed on. I groped through the dark until I felt heavy velvet curtains, pushed them aside and found myself under the glare of a sodium floodlight. A Chinese voice came over a loud PA system: "Now Manager Yang Si-An [my Chinese name] will say a few words!" In the glare, I could barely make out the audience, but I could sense there were a few hundred people there. They stood and applauded. I was terrified, but it seemed I was the keynoter, so I managed to stutter a few words about how much US investors welcomed China's rise.

After my "speech", I walked through the exhibits. There were bio-engineered seeds for a new type of apple, a ball-bearing that the inventor claimed was novel, some kind of circuit board, fertiliser made from charred wood, and much more. Everyone was looking for foreign investment in order to scale up production. I had none to offer, and I worried these innovators could see I was a fraud. But then it dawned on me: my employer's "host organisation" had fulfilled a favour to the factory managers by putting them in front of me; the factory managers had got a free trip to the provincial capital, and I had fulfilled an obligation to the host by coming. No one expected any actual business to come out of it.

In the early years of "reform and opening", I was frequently treated as a prize zoo animal: any white person randomly appearing in a city was automatically seen as an avatar of business shrewdness and put on display. At a conference in Henan, I was asked to sit next to the governor for a television interview: the other foreigners at the conference, from Africa and India, were seated out of sight in the back, since I was considered higher status; it was thought that white Americans and Europeans had the most investment to offer.

The whole nation mobilised to appear more hospitable to foreigners. Elderly leaders swapped their Mao suits for Western sports jackets. They went abroad and learned English. Within China, foreigners were the first to get phones at home and access to cable TV with English-language stations. Foreigners had special licence plates and never got traffic tickets. They got privileged access to government leaders. A foreign visitor to a city in the provinces would be showered with gifts and feted at banquets. In the capital, the most lowly foreign factory manager could meet with a high official of state and be treated like Henry Kissinger, provided an official interpreter, and earnestly asked his or her view about the economy while beautiful young women replenished the jasmine tea in lidded enamel cups. Everywhere, we were treated as special. Crowds would follow me if I walked through towns outside the capital, and children would chant *"lao wei!"* (foreigner). Chinese everywhere were charmingly open about the problems of their country and admiring of the West. When pushing my son around in a carriage in the early years, people would stop me on the street and say, "He will be very smart and very handsome. He has American blood!"

This sort of special treatment charmed and bemused foreigners, who failed to see that Chinese people viewed them as walking bags of money. Here was a government that had changed seemingly overnight from closed, suspicious, internally tyrannical, and externally belligerent to one that actively, disarmingly solicited foreign investment and trade and seemed to offer new freedoms to its businesses. China was shedding the restrictions and prohibitions of the Maoist era like a suit of clothes in warm weather. It felt as if the entire nation had awoken from the Maoist slumber and wanted to make up for lost time.

The creeping capitalism following the "reform and opening" of 1979 took root in the mid- to late 1980s and made Beijing look like a film going from black-and-white to colour. Every time you went to the market, there would be something new – bananas from the Philippines, pineapples, peanut oil. Dreary urban markets selling cabbage and potatoes burst into cornucopias of fruits, vegetables, and meats. Where timid customers once had to beg "comrade" store clerks to sell them long underwear or a shirt in the only available colour, pale blue, suddenly there were hypermarkets exploding with colourful knit sweaters and blouses. People began to eat better, dress better, skip political study sessions, and even get Saturdays off. Ration coupons disappeared, and so did the ever-present fear of saying something the Party might not like. There started to be dances, music, real films, and books of poetry.

All of this change, choice, and freedom was intoxicating. It lasted a long time, and those ¥60 pay packets got fatter, until Chinese people could imagine buying cars and electronics and going overseas for fun. The rules that had kept people tethered to their employers were dispensed with, and people went looking for jobs they preferred with people they found compatible. Jobs were easy to find, at escalating wages, and parents saw their children moving far beyond their own stations in life. The rapid improvements lulled everyone, Chinese and foreign, into believing that China could never return to the bad old days.

That turned out to be an illusion.

✳

China's open arms for Western business created a system whereby corporate managers, and later, bankers, could persuade the owners of capital to invest in China for "access" and "growth" rather than profit. The self-interest of these financial gatekeepers merged with their belief that Chinese bureaucrats held the keys to the market and might withhold access if at all displeased. They lavished praise on China and its leaders. Their faith in China's rapid progress was continually affirmed by the changing physical landscape; it was said that, in the mid-1990s, 20 per cent of the working cranes in the world could be found in the coastal "Tier 1" city of Shanghai. No one paid much attention to standards of health and education or to human rights: a rising tide floats all boats.

It took me years to understand that I was an unwitting player in an elaborate dramatic confection. This country, which had seemed so malleable, so interested in change, was actually a sprawling, ancient kingdom with deeply ingrained traditions indifferent to the proselytisers of capitalism. Foreign visitors and residents stayed within the tiny foreign districts that nestled in Tier 1 cities like snow globes in the palm of a hand. Those zones contained some of the best hotels in the world and the best-paved roads leading to huge airports with the newest aircraft. Foreigners woke up on crisp white sheets and sipped freshly squeezed orange juice from lounges overlooking the city, then folded their copies of the *Financial Times* and headed downstairs to black chauffeur-driven Audis. This was the China foreign investors visited and remarked on, but it was actually a brightly lit Wunderkammer, a cabinet of curiosities on display for a hand-picked audience of bankers and consultants, corporate executives, journalists, and diplomats who could open the door, have a glimpse, and report to the rest of the world that the Chinese cabinets were surprisingly well-stocked. After all, visas were hard to get, and backpacker types were not welcome.

Illusive though it was, the illuminated cabinet was an exciting place to live. It was easy to become an entrepreneur, and I started a publishing company, a CRM software company, then an online media company in rapid succession. Foreign investors and clients welcomed these businesses as footholds in the vast and confusing local terrain.

By then, as well as a husband, I had two children and an older stepson, a big extended family, a dog, a house, and two cars. Our family lived in a foreign neighbourhood that might have been "Mayberry", where we wheeled around on bicycles, stopped for espresso machiatto at Starbucks, and shopped at a grocery store selling foreign goods like Italian basil and dishwasher powder – unknown in Chinese households. We roasted a turkey at Thanksgiving even though the imported bird cost more than our couch. We enjoyed the freedom to watch foreign movies (albeit pirated), attend church, and hold sports events – freedoms that Chinese people did not have.

Few foreigners ventured outside the bubble of Shunyi – the residential district for foreigners in Beijing – or Chaoyang, where businesses and embassies sit. But a Sunday trip just 50 kilometres west would expose a China unchanged from 300 years earlier. Barefoot children in the Mentougou district were grateful for donations of pencils and schoolbags from Beijing's foreign churches. In Chengde, a resort near Beijing, beggars would surround anyone ordering a bowl of soup at a local restaurant. Vacation spots north of the city offered filthy squat toilets, unheated interiors, and nothing to do unless one wanted to visit local prostitutes.

We rationalised the disparities because we assumed all the construction under way would gradually lift these places out of poverty. But rapid and stunning changes to the physical landscape did little to improve access to healthcare, education, or to provide social mobility for the great majority. Culturally and legally, meanwhile, China was becoming darker and more limited. When the Olympics came around, the darkness could no longer be ignored.

The 2008 Olympic Games were just the sort of event that would send the Chinese leadership into paroxysmal anxiety. The world would be watching. Every bureaucracy was warned there could be no mistakes, and the best way to avoid them was to limit all possible activity. Hotels that had renovated in anticipation of visitors for the Games found they were not allowed to take foreign guests. Applications for visas were rejected. Internet controls were stepped up to an operatic level, such that news like the death of babies from drinking contaminated milk powder was suppressed, with the milk remaining available. Hundreds of thousands of people were deputised to monitor speech and patrol gatherings.

China is a sprawling country with weak vertical authority, and it often relies on quotas to achieve targets. This is true in law enforcement as well as the economy. In the run-up to the Olympics, police were given such high arrest quotas that they relied on third-party agents to help them find people to arrest. This arrangement quickly morphed into a for-profit enterprise involving what amounted to an extra-legal kidnapping and ransom process with payments for release that started at around US$50,000. I personally knew a half dozen people arrested under this scheme. One couple sold their house to pay the fees, then quickly returned to the US for good.

The cultural environment was no less constricted. After 2008, arts events became high-priced performances by visiting artists whose concerts had to be approved at top levels and only for very short runs. The constricted availability of foreign films in cinemas contrasted with the wide distribution of pirated DVDs.

The Olympic experience brought me to understand that China had not changed institutionally, and that the post-1979 experiment with capitalism was just that: an experiment that, when deemed to be no longer useful, would be discarded. The Communist Party opened up to the providers of capital, and having collected enough cash, began to retreat from international involvement.

Just as China has turned away from its earnest wooing of the West, so the West has become disillusioned with China. Back in the early reform era, the Wunderkammer constructed by China's political elite worked well to create a conceptual framework for the rest of the world. China was viewed as the Little Nation That Could, where a bright young brain trust was quietly transforming an old-time socialist economy into a capitalist one and acting as midwife to an emerging Jeffersonian democracy. The self-interest of foreign-capital gatekeepers dovetailed with the Chinese leadership's interest in keeping money flowing. From 1980 to about 2015, when capital flows to China slowed and started to reverse, the world applied an analytic framework to China that grew increasingly distant from the truth.

The West mistook Chinese reforms for an alteration of its governing system. Western nations' hopes and anxieties were equally projected onto the Chinese screen. Those fears have emerged every few years around a different aspect of China's "rise" and the economic and political threat felt by workers and companies in the US and Europe. After China acceded to the World Trade Organization, the West believed that China's indigenous innovation drive might obliterate foreign technology companies. Endless conferences were held on China's technological ambitions. Around 2014, as China was pitching to make its currency part of mandatory international reserves, economists worried that the renminbi would overtake the dollar as the preferred currency of world trade and investment. Then, after Russia invaded Ukraine, analysts opined that China was building a new world order in competition with the US. None of these fears have been realised, yet two quite different constituencies internationally continue to stress the reality closest to their own interests: competitive, threatening China or admirable, cooperative China; one growing into a belligerent threat to world peace, the other encompassing a vast new market, which no foreign company can afford to ignore.

Actually, neither view is accurate. The fear of China as a competitor is misplaced. But understanding China's effects on the world economy and governance has only just begun. Offshoring industries and manufacturing to China hammered prices in the West and reduced the negotiating power of labour. Whole cities in the United States and Europe have been hollowed out, with the predictable social problems that follow the departure of jobs. Western political systems have found themselves ill-equipped to govern companies operating outside their jurisdictions, and the massive profits realised by corporations and Western bankers in China, instead of being invested in needed infrastructure back home, have filled the pockets of corporate barons. The emergence of China as an economic power has been coincident with the rise of billionaire oligarchs. The West has suffered a crisis of faith in democracy and has tilted towards authoritarianism. Without being China's fault, all these international effects are associated with China's emergence in the global economy.

The story of the Chinese nation generally is one of hopes raised, whether by peasant revolution, the opening of foreign trade, or the Communist vision, and then dashed, when a ruling elite secures its position and closes off the paths to prosperity and freedom for the majority. In the early days, many people joined the Chinese revolution out of idealism, but idealists want a voice, and the dictatorial system that Chinese communism soon became does not brook even the most timid form of dissent. Euphoria characterised the early revolutionary period, but it wasn't long before the Party, allied to Stalin, demonstrated that its own continued power was more important than the well-being of the people.

The tendency of an elite to cling to power is of course the Achilles' heel of any political system, but a one-party system like China's has no self-correcting mechanisms. That is why we see China now on a return path to poverty and isolation. The Communist Party seeks isolation from international pressure to implement institutional change because it wants unchallenged rule over its people. The effects of China's retraction into its historical state as a mysterious and recondite kingdom will be tragic for the Chinese people. And the effects on the rest of the world will be as momentous. Like a film being run backwards, as much as China's integration into the world economy changed lives across the world, so will its shrinkage and retraction.

CHAPTER ONE

COMING OUT
THE FIRST DECADE (1979–88)

To understand how far China has come since it emerged, blinking, from three decades of Maoist isolation, we need to be reminded of what the country was like when reforms began, in 1979. Personal freedoms were non-existent. People were not allowed to travel without permission, to marry, to have a child, or to be buried. A moment of carelessness – for example, using a newspaper that had a photograph of Chairman Mao printed on it to wrap fish – could lead to imprisonment or even death. Economically, China had been dramatically under-invested for decades. While nearby countries like Japan and South Korea changed from quasi-medieval regions into modern states, China remained a nation where meat was a once-a-week luxury, cooking was done outside using coal briquettes half made of mud, and even in the capital city, residents had to use public toilets from which labourers shovelled excrement weekly into "honey wagons" that donkeys pulled to the city outskirts, where it was used to fertilise crops. Roads, railways, and ports were pathetically sparse. Capital was so scarce that Mao's drive to make steel required people to melt down the spatulas they used for cooking.

Only Chairman Mao, who had led the nation to victory over the Japanese and then over the Nationalists, had the personal authority capable of making people tolerate such poverty and hardship. Even so, to sustain his own power, he had to use young, fanatical Red Guard supporters to launch a civil war that lasted from 1966 to his death in 1976. When the chairman, his brain riddled with dementia, died, his wife and three other true believers, dubbed the Gang of Four, made a bid to keep the Cultural Revolution alive, but the four were deposed in a palace coup. Mao's imprisoned wife, Jiang Qing, became a perverse symbol of heroism. Before (reportedly) taking her own life, she defiantly railed against those who had put her in prison. "Just release me, and in half a year, I'll eliminate the lot of you."

The country drifted. Hua Guofeng, a weak and mild-mannered politician with a receding chin and a buck-toothed smile that somehow made its owner look like he was pleading for approval, took over, declaring that China would continue on the Maoist path. But it was a brief interregnum; the nation was more than ready to move on. Hua was manoeuvred out by Deng Xiaoping, fresh out of prison.

The forceful and plain-talking Deng ascended and launched an economic revolution. Affectionately called "Comrade Xiaoping" – it is a rare sign of familiarity in

China to use an elder's given name – five-foot-two Deng was shaped like a fire hydrant and had the chain-smoking, floor-spitting ways of Chinese from the country. Deng set out to bring in hard foreign currency to enable imports; to make industry more efficient; then to reduce rural poverty.

Hard currency came first, and the strategies, both political and economic, were ingenious. Deng became acutely aware of the shortage of hard currency when he decided to visit the United States, meet with President Jimmy Carter, and hang out with the pop teen idol Donny Osmond: it turned out China didn't have money for the airfare and hotel charges. China's currency, the renminbi, was and still is "soft", meaning it can't be used outside the country – even in Hong Kong or Macao. Dollars to pay for dinners in Washington, flights between cities, and hotel costs could come only from export earnings. In the book *Red Capitalism*, Carl Walter and Fraser Howie recount the story that Deng, trying to rustle up money for the trip, ordered an inventory of hard currency among all of China's banks and came up with…US$38,000 – hardly enough for a large delegation, even in 1979.

It is not known how many people accompanied Deng on his weeklong trip, but the Chinese somehow managed to pay for necessities. That did not diminish the urgency of the currency shortage. China successfully kept its people from buying things that would have required hard currency, like television sets, refrigerators, Marlboro cigarettes. Even Chinese brands that had an export market, like Tsingtao and Kweichow Moutai, could not be had for love or money. The Flying Pigeon bicycle, which had a slightly better reputation than the ubiquitous Phoenix brand, could be purchased only at a hard-currency Friendship Store, which Chinese people were not allowed to enter without special permission.

3

But if China was to develop exports, companies would need to import components, and that required dollars. Deng knew it would be necessary to allow foreigners and their capital into the country. Foreign companies would ensure that products made at factories in China would have a ready market, because the companies themselves would buy them for sale overseas. For Coca-Cola and Levi Strauss and Sara Lee, dollars were just the way you paid for things; for China, dollars were precious.

China needed their currency and so had to allow foreigners in, but these aliens represented a threat. To keep foreigners from morally polluting the Chinese people, Deng boxed off the new, more open economy into test-tube zones that would generate wealth more efficiently than in the socialist economy but whose freer ways would be segregated from the rest of the country. He made this noncontroversial by carving out of physical locations, laws, institutions, and staff who would be dedicated to the new commercial economy, keeping the new zones, their people, and legal system hermetically sealed off so as not to disturb the overall political system.

This legal separation expressed itself in an elaborate system of quarantine that included the Open Coastal Cities programme, the Special Economic Zones, the establishment of distinct agencies to be the employers of record for any Chinese working with foreigners, and the writing of new laws to govern foreign-invested companies, starting with the Joint Venture Law of 1979. The whole bureaucracy had arranged itself so as to place a thick membrane between foreigners and Chinese: foreign nationals were required to live in special compounds managed by special bureaucracies, they had separate medical facilities, and they used a separate currency. Romantic relationships were forbidden between foreigners and Chinese, and suspicion would fall on any Chinese who had a personal relationship with a foreigner; not only would they be watched by security personnel, but their peers would think they were somehow selling out the motherland for personal advantage. One middle-aged American in Shanghai who had teenage, Chinese-looking daughters bitterly complained that when he was out with them without his wife, people would follow them on the street yelling, "Traitors! Whores!" at the girls.

The incentives were all about capturing hard-currency investment. In most cases, the special zones were managed by newly incorporated entities operating under delegated authority, acting as quasi-governments. The zone managers, who held civil service rank, were advanced or rewarded on the basis of meeting targets focused on the scale of capital investment and gross tax revenues. That incentivised everyone to bring in as much money as possible. Moving a factory from a city centre to a special zone might have undermined the business overall, but it brought turnover to the zone. No one thought about whether the investment created jobs or in some other way benefited the average person living in the area. And it worked: investment poured in. Visiting Western managers loved to remark on China's business-friendly atmosphere, not like home, where you had to endure tiresome public hearings before getting anything built.

CAPITALIST ZONES

China has relied on a patchwork of special legal and territorial concessions for most of its modern history – the Maoist era excepted – to enable economic growth without changing the core institutions that manage most of the mainland's territory. There was Macao ruled by Portugal from the Ming dynasty; Hong Kong, ruled by Britain; and a dozen foreign concessions operated by Japan, Germany, the United States, and other countries in the late Qing and Republican periods. The brilliant innovation of Deng Xiaoping was to turn this not-in, not-out system to China's advantage by making it serve not the trading desires of foreign countries but China's own need for exports.

In 1980, Shenzhen was a fishing village that lay just steps from Hong Kong. The area had been deliberately kept empty as a buffer, lest some of the capitalism, licentiousness, and neon lights seeped over the border from the then-British colony. Under Deng, Shenzhen became the first and most successful "special zone". It was one of three designated by Deng in 1980 to process goods for export. Shenzhen, Zhuhai, and, up the coast, Shantou, were chosen for their proximity to areas of Chinese irredentist interest: Hong Kong, Macao, and Taiwan, respectively. All three areas are in politically powerful Guangdong (transliterated as "Canton" before Mao came along), a key military base for China. Xiamen, in Fujian Province, directly across the strait from Taiwan, quickly followed in being designated a Special Economic Zone or "SEZ", and the island of Hainan, not yet a province, became the fifth.

Deng established Shenzhen as a sort of translation tool between British-ruled Hong Kong and the mainland, enabling the benefits of both systems to fuel growth. On the mainland side of Shenzhen grew an almost slave-like manufacturing behemoth, with tides of cheap labour pouring into the city from the hinterland to make every manner of thing for export. On the side of Shenzhen nearest to Hong Kong was the skilled trading and banking capacity of a highly regarded, rule-of-law financial centre that would finance mainland growth, upgrade design and manufacturing capability, and facilitate rapid expansion of export trade. Hong Kong maintained separate rules for customs and tariffs; banking, finance, and currency; taxes; corruption, due process, habeas corpus; and much more. As such, Hong Kong functioned as a way to leverage the liberal financial order of the West against the closed system of the Chinese mainland, enabling the tariff evasion and financial capers that have made China the investment-friendly place that Russia has never been.

Given that fixed residence permits determine where an individual in China is allowed to live, China has developed an enormous pool of seasonal workers who move to cities unaccompanied by their families. In the 1980s, workers could not move to Shenzhen without a job, and a job meant a factory that would house them in a dormitory and feed them in a cafeteria, keeping them working more or less around the clock. The rigid controls around travel to Shenzhen were eventually relaxed, but to this day, China maintains a system of healthcare, education, and welfare that makes it impossible or at least very expensive and perilous to raise a family away from one's registered home. Lacking an official *hukou* or residence permit, which would designate them as legal urban residents, internal migrant workers in China are treated much like undocumented immigrants in the United States or Europe.

The abolition of rules that applied to the rest of China was a massive contributor to Shenzhen's growth. In 1984, now a city, Shenzhen began to issue "temporary residence certificates", meaning that migrants from inland provinces could reside there legally as long as they could find a job. By 1988, the majority of Shenzhen's population came from other parts of the country. Given its cosmopolitan nature, Shenzhen needed to use nationally recognised currency, and it became the first city to abolish the food coupon system, allowing residents to buy food with money instead of the chits issued by local governments. Shenzhen in 1987 also introduced China's first fixed-term grant of land-use rights, to the China National Aero-Technology Import & Export Corp. The city was the first to implement labour-contract rules. And there was much more in the way of innovation. People flocked to the city, seeking economic opportunity and a freer way of life.

No other territory enjoyed as much policy flexibility. Perhaps the master key to Shenzhen's success has been the presence of China's military, in business as well as defence. The military could provide special access to Hong Kong visitor permits, a special quota for passports and the right to settle abroad for executives of Shenzhen enterprises under military control, as well as access to grain and oil that made abolition of rationing coupons feasible, and special rights to land. The military demobilisation and falling defence budgets of the mid-1980s also contributed to Shenzhen's development, because demobilised soldiers needed to go somewhere, and many of them took over companies that had been run by the military.

Territorial concessions had always allowed different rules for foreigners, but here was a city in which select Chinese people lived under a distinct legal regime. Shenzhen trembled between the austerity of the mainland and the freedoms of Hong Kong, something like a soufflé hastily removed from the oven. But with Shenzhen's help, freer practices became

8

ensconced and legitimated, even if they did not spread to the interior.

Thus rules-based Hong Kong and the "special" territory of Shenzhen invisibly collaborated to create a vast grey zone in which raw capitalism thrived. Whether not-in, not-out territories like Hong Kong or special zones on the mainland, the combination of sovereign power and its expression through multiple systems served China's reforms very well.

EXPORT MACHINE

Shenzhen and the other special zones were designed to promote exports, the first thrust of China's development push, without undergoing the uniform regulatory changes that would otherwise have been necessary. The exporting cities and the factories they contained were built around ports, and the workers they hired came from the inland provinces. In some cases, the exporting zones like Shenzhen were chosen specifically because they were empty, with very small native populations.

The zones were also set up to facilitate technology transfer from overseas, assembling imported parts for export as finished goods. The export-processing system had been introduced largely to overcome the anti-export bias created by the state-managed trading system and the fixed exchange rate. At the time, foreigners had to use a special currency that traded at three to the dollar, much pricier than the value one could get on the street for the same foreign exchange certificates. Once "swap" markets emerged, the unofficial rate went over eight to the dollar, so official exports at three to one were exceedingly unattractive.

But currency wasn't the only impediment. Firms producing for export sold their products to monopoly, state-owned foreign-trade companies at officially determined prices. The producers did not get the hard currency from the international sale of their products, nor could they adjust prices up when they encountered strong demand, so they had little incentive to expand production. All of this meant China did not realise the benefit of exporting labour-intensive goods. The export-processing system started to change this by providing a wide array of incentives to companies in the zones. They could import parts and raw materials duty-free, as long as the finished goods were exported, and that created a huge boost. Companies were finally permitted to charge international prices rather than the prices set in Beijing.

The export-processing trade was pioneered by textile and garment producers. Manufacturers of all manner of light-industrial goods, from toys to telecommunications equipment, followed. In short order, China became the largest exporter of clothing, toys, machinery, and consumer electronics in the world. The system also helped generate an employment boom. By the turn of the twenty-first century, export processing accounted for half of all China's trade, and by 2005, 58 per cent of China's exports came from the special zones.

By the early 1980s, the economy was running on a dual-track system: many companies continued to operate within the government's plan, but the prices of a few commodities were permitted to rise, and private businesses could sometimes sell them. New outdoor stalls offered goods unavailable through the state stores, at higher prices.

Because this de-control process was spreading to a wider range of product categories, there was ambiguity around what was and was not permissible. Many companies continued to enjoy the security of being "in plan" but could also augment incomes by producing more and selling it through the "free market". Suddenly, there was an explosion of branded products selling at low prices in the "open markets" — factories making Burberry coats or Beanie Babies toys just made a few more than had been ordered and supplemented their incomes. Naturally, everyone wanted to try a hand at creating a cottage industry within the confines of a state company or a secure government job. There was inexorable pressure for the free-market experiments to expand in scope.

CITY TO COUNTRY

The next prong of the Dengist reforms was a rural revolution designed to emancipate agricultural China from requirements that farmers produce only what they were told to and sell their grain or oil or hogs at a pre-determined price. Farmers had chafed under the system that had Party officials in Beijing determining what, how, and when they should plant, disregarding local conditions that farmers understood far better than the bureaucrats did. The relaxation unleashed astonishing growth.

First, the government altered the requirement that farmers grow only staple crops like rice and wheat. Instead, authorities issued quotas, after satisfaction of which farmers could grow what they pleased and sell the surplus in newly established "open markets". With the money they made, they established small companies. Since private ownership was still not recognised, the companies were set up under village ownership and designated "township and village enterprises" or TVEs. These companies made all sorts of things planners had not anticipated a need for – trash bags, collapsible umbrellas, colourful clothing, sunglasses. Availability bred desire, which bred availability, until the new "free markets" popping up in the cities teemed with goods that would have been considered frivolous only a year or two earlier.

Entrepreneurial businesses started in the coastal provinces, without clear property rights, but with sufficient support they virtually exploded: the output of rural industries increased by 26 per cent every year between 1979 and 1987, and rural incomes grew rapidly – by nearly 12 per cent annually in real terms. For a time, household income grew much faster than GDP, and consumption also grew as a proportion of GDP. People who had been doing subsistence farming were able to raise capital and start small businesses to make toys, bras, snack foods, whatever. This was mostly a coastal phenomenon, and regions varied: in some, the new entrepreneurial businesses were allowed to grow unimpeded; in others, there was a good deal of bureaucratic interference and control.

Some provinces took to the new entrepreneurial systems with lightning speed. According to the MIT professor Huang Yasheng, by the end of 1981, 98 per cent of the households in Guizhou Province had adopted agricultural contracting, meaning they signed a contract to farm a particular plot of land (rather than join a team farming collective land) and guaranteed delivery to state procurement offices of a fixed amount of grain, while they could sell any surplus for cash. Contract farming had become nearly universal by the end of 1983, causing grain production to surge. Farmers started to use their free time to work at small businesses.

The planning system could not always keep up with this growth. Raw materials could not be appropriately allocated, staff were in short supply, and money came up short, as the government had to shift from expropriation of all company proceeds to taxation. In many industries, bureaucrats could not wrap their heads around a new and alien system. If a company wanted to open a higher-price dining hall for employees, for example, it might be permitted to do that as long as it did not demand in-plan supplies of food and cooks to work the kitchens.

As funding weakened, so did regulatory oversight; the ministries had no choice but to step back, and this retreat in itself enabled businesses to grow. The computer company Lenovo, for example, started when restrictions on selling computers were loosened; the founders of Lenovo (then called Legend) started as distributors for IBM computers.

The third and most radical prong of the Dengist reforms, one that had deep and unanticipated effects, involved letting energetic individuals take over the operation of state companies.

PRIVATISATION

At the start of the reform period in 1979, Chinese business was directly owned, financed, and managed by government agencies. The following decade saw the government devise a series of mechanisms to shift business towards independent management and private participation. While government agencies retained the levers of ultimate control, they stepped back in order to realise higher benefits and, in the process, handed out limited franchise rights for private parties to participate in managing the wealth they would create.

Diverse mechanisms were deployed. In one common strategy, ministries contracted out (*chengbao*) the operation and financing of state companies to private parties, which undertook payment of all operating expenses in return for the right to keep profits. Starting in the late 1980s, government-owned investment funds were established to finance companies and receive the rights to cash flows without directly managing the businesses. The "limited by shares" corporate structure permitted mixed public and private ownership. Bureaucratically imposed mergers enabled failing companies to benefit from cross-subsidisation with profitable ones. Under these diverse formats, political leaders and government institutions retained a high degree of control over an economy that was quietly privatising.

Key to the economic development that took off in the 1980s was the devolution of decision-making to lower levels of government, with less oversight. This had two effects: it accelerated the economy and it also created windfall earnings for the new government allies. In the meantime, the growth of government agencies lagged behind the proliferation of commercial entities, such that regulators had to move back from direct micromanagement of companies and develop methods of governance that would allow a smaller number of people to regulate more companies.

Before 1980, companies had virtually no discretionary financial resources. The profit-retention system instantly altered the incentives in industry but also reduced government revenue sharply, as there was no change to controlled prices. As companies kept more of the proceeds of their businesses and gave less to government, property rights remained vague and shifting, creating more incentive to exploit state property for private gain.

Meanwhile, as government revenue fell, the economy became more firmly tethered to capital investment as an engine of growth, relying more on the banking system as its key utility to drive investment capital to the industries and regions it deemed most advantageous.

The print media provides a vivid illustration of how even small new incentives led to wild growth that challenged the system.

For a Westerner who arrived in China in the 1980s, the publishing industry was like something from before Gutenberg's time: newsprint was scarce; the post office, the monopoly distributor of newspapers and magazines, was uninterested in timely home delivery; and daily newspapers were read from noticeboards protected by glass cases on each city's broadest avenues. Official newspapers, bought via mandatory subscription by all government companies and organisations, were generally brief and contained didactic editorials about issues distant from the average person's life, like the visit of an African state leader or the agricultural achievements of a certain locality. Protocol was obsessively observed: the first 500 words of a report on a national celebration would list all the officials who attended in order of rank, attaching all their titles. This recital would contain hints about the current political standing of the leaders so subtle that combing the grammar and usage for hidden comments became a national pastime. Newspapers, carrying instructive messages from the Party, formed the syllabus for Saturday "study groups" at all Chinese companies, schools, and government offices.

Newspapers were not for recreational reading. Even

15

today, articles about soccer matches, for example, are tightly controlled lest they incite violence. Gossip magazines are rare, since it is hard to figure out what will cross a political line; exposing personal information about political leaders is strictly forbidden, and film and music stars often get into trouble when they become too prominent. The only lively star coverage is of business leaders, and airport bookshops try to bring in customers by playing videos of famous businesspeople talking about how to be successful.

As the state began to retreat, the print media started to solicit advertising and subscription revenue. Quasi-private publications, suddenly able to sustain themselves without subsidies from a supervising ministry, proliferated. The regulatory system accommodated economic growth by splitting media content into three sections. One part is delivered by the Party's propaganda bureau and must be run verbatim – the lead articles in *People's Daily*, for example, which retain the stilted character of the old, coded texts. The second category of content is looser and may be generated by journalists but must be approved by censors, while the third category, free content, confines itself to safe topics such as relationships, entertainment, and feats of heroism by Party and military officials. Publishing content that steps outside hazy ideological boundaries is punished retroactively but harshly, leading publications – and now internet media – to work hard at self-censorship.

The first phase of media growth came in the early 1980s, as subsidies were being gradually withdrawn. At the period of highest growth around 1984, a new newspaper appeared roughly every four days. Over the decade of the 1980s, the number of China's newspapers grew from 186 to nearly 2,000; magazines from a few hundred to more than 7,000;

TV stations from about 700 to around 9,000, although that number includes more than 5,000 cable networks run by state-owned companies or housing compounds.

The easiest way to go into business in the media in the early 1980s was to do it under the wing of the government. The period from 1980 to 1984 saw huge growth in the publications sponsored by government ministries, a class of publications the West would call "trades" that in theory covered topics of interest to ministry employees, like a magazine about heavy machinery for the Ministry of Machine Building or coal mines for the Ministry of Coal. Private operators stretched the definition of the trade titles they took on, publishing, for example, a cooking magazine as an "internal" title for the Ministry of Light Industry. These magazines enjoyed relatively little ideological and Party oversight and were supposedly limited to "internal" circulation within a ministry – although in fact they circulated like any conventional magazine or newspaper. These were subsidised by the ministries that owned them. Ultimately, the central government grew displeased and in 1986 commissioned the People's University to conduct a survey of publications, concluding that most new publications should not be on the government tab. Ministries were told to cut off the subsidies.

The withdrawal of funding unleashed an era of intense media competition. Publications grew in size and variety and began to seek more muscular distribution strategies. Quasi-legal distribution organisations grew up at the city and provincial level to compete with the postal system. Star journalists emerged on the staff of prominent dailies. A commercial advertising market emerged, but circulation was the most important driver of revenue. Competing for circulation, newspapers and magazines began to publish articles on divorce, shoddy products, and the plight of the average Chinese faced with job competition and government layoffs. The liberalised content was a challenge to the Party, which was concerned with maintaining control over the flow of information.

Even more challenging was the weakening of the state's distribution monopoly. China's founding premier, the beloved Zhou Enlai, had set up the post office as monopoly distributor of publications because the postal system has grass-roots reach and therefore could play an important role in organising and propagandising the population. Door-to-door delivery was a channel for political communication, so when independent organisations started doing it, the government got extremely nervous.

The post office's monopoly was not only politically important, it was also lucrative. The post office collected 35 to 40 per cent of the cover price of a magazine or newspaper from the publisher as its distribution fee. But the post office grew less and less efficient in the new publication environment: publications got heavier, subscribers more fragmented, and rural distribution more onerous. The cover-price proposition became less attractive.

Meanwhile, the business had become very competitive, and readers demanded timeliness. Urban-based publications began establishing their own distribution networks, by poaching postal employees while building political strategies to fend off the inevitable attacks, as they ate the post office's lunch. In 1996, *Beijing Youth Daily* established its own distribution company, Little Red Cap (sometimes translated as "Little Red Riding Hood"), by hiring members of the Post Office Publication Distribution division at high salaries, handing out bicycles (then a coveted commodity), and getting the managers to set up a network of bicycle messengers.

Red Cap reached an agreement with the Bank of Industry and Commerce to have subscription fees accepted at any branch, which solved the problem of consumer trust (no one wanted to hand cash to the messengers) and took the financing stream out of the hands of the post office. The model was replicated around the country – there was a Little Blue Cap, a Little Yellow Cap, and every time the post office appealed to political authorities to restore the cash cow of distribution, the periodicals would claim that they were providing a needed source of urban employment for people who were being laid off from factories. Since the post office reports to the central authorities and employment is a local responsibility, local officials protected the start-ups, and the post office watched this revenue stream seep away.

By the end of the 1980s, economic reforms had engendered a regulatory shift, from direct, pre-publication content control to after-the-fact penalties for offensive content. Instead of having all periodicals delivered by one reliable bureaucracy, newspapers had their own delivery crews. Some of these also started delivering advertising, commercial samples, and even surveys. This sort of direct access to individuals, without the mediation of a Party organ, was completely new to the system and very challenging to say the least.

This disorderly and uneven growth of businesses and opportunities is what made life in China in the 1980s exciting. People who had made modest incomes as drivers or repairmen suddenly made more money than anyone had ever imagined possible. People who would otherwise need to spend decades working to gain authority in a state industry were being offered jobs with high levels of responsibility at high salaries. It seemed that anything was possible. At the same time, the hybrid economy created arbitrage opportunities, corruption, a sharp divergence of opportunity for people with connections to the state versus those without, and bursts of rapid inflation.

With businesses growing like weeds, the Party started to lose control. This happened in several ways. First, government agencies had to step back and adopt more rules-based regulatory strategies because they simply did not have the personnel to oversee all the new companies. The old system of one censor dedicated to each publication could not continue. Next, companies found ways to capture funding without applying to their hidebound supervising ministries, and once they could get capital, they paid a lot less attention to their ministerial overlords.

Newfound freedoms led to pressure for more autonomy. The government established new, often ad hoc, corporate structures to enable growth. At the start of reforms, China recognised only factories and offices. Companies could not manage multiple locations or consolidate money or inventory even within one city, much less across regions. But by the end of the 1980s, companies were beginning to operate as integrated organisations.

One of the most momentous changes was the emergence of a fused political and corporate elite. As more money began to circulate outside of the ministries, investment capital was sprung free of direct bureaucratic control. At the same time, China was developing its first stock market and was also packaging its greatest state monopolies to raise money on public markets. The stock markets promised access to capital without the strings that foreign direct investors attached, and they promised capital gains of a scope not previously imagined.

Devolution of control over investment decisions to lower levels of government allowed money to flow more readily. This entailed improving the incentive system by providing tacit approval of corrupt gains. Local officials in the early years, for example, received a commission on capital raised from private investors. By mid-1980, there were thousands of enterprises enrolled in the "profit retention" plan, allowing them to keep 70 per cent of profit and distribute it as bonuses, creating powerful new incentives to increase sales.

These strategies initially worked like a charm. Desultory peasants required to grow rice in unsuited soil turned their land to cash crops like tea and fruit and built themselves houses from the proceeds. Dusty electronics factories sold "shares" to the public to raise expansion capital. Unused factories restarted. Functionally bankrupt facilities were taken over by their managers and turned into export powerhouses.

SHARING THE WEALTH

All this entrepreneurial energy created a burst of growth that benefited just about everyone in China. After decades of a winter diet consisting of cabbage and rice, Beijingers found that exotic southern fruits were appearing in private stalls. Supermarkets opened, allowing shoppers to pick their items off open shelves instead of begging a stolid counter clerk to fetch something they wanted. People would put on their best clothes to visit but not buy, as everything was much more expensive than it was in street markets. Visitors were astounded that clerks in these new stores were not walking the aisles to check browsers for theft. Clothing became abundant and more various; no longer was there just a single colour and single size, one for men and one for women. Amazingly, a few birthday cakes appeared, though many days old and with white frosting that tasted like shaving cream. A few lucky households managed to install telephones. Life improved, in both little ways and big. In the 1980s, it felt like the whole nation had woken up on Christmas morning to see consumer abundance under the tree and realised that the world was not, after all, the sinister place of Dickensian horrors that the Party had been warning about.

The wealth spurt was a political necessity as well as a bold leadership choice. Deng Xiaoping, after all, was a capitalist roader, rehabilitated and brought back to Beijing on forbearance. Deng's "moderate" faction provided support for reforms, but he also needed support from highly placed political and military figures who had been pushed aside and persecuted in more radical times.

The best tool Deng had for securing this support was the economy, and the limited rights doled out in the early years directly benefited those people the new Deng government needed. There was a short list of companies, for example, entitled to keep a portion of their profit for reinvestment. Franchises could be handed to military allies in certain Special Economic Zones, and there was more investment capital that could be spent at the discretion of provincial officials, provided that they supported Deng. The reforms, therefore, were the seedbed of China's red elite, a class that over the following decade became kleptocrats at a level the world had never seen before.

The critical tool to enable these benefits was capital, and the principal means of accumulating capital was exports.

Accordingly, the new regulatory regime emerging in the early 1980s focused on creating exports and keeping the resulting hard-currency earnings at home.

The attempt to segregate the freer economy from the "real" China failed miserably. Economic expansion had created a series of crisis points. In a brief few years, Chinese urban society had developed the tools and communication channels for political protest. The breakdown of state planning belied the hope that the Party could contain the capitalist portion of the economy separate from most of Chinese society, like uranium inside a lead box. Instead, the private economy was radiating beyond its designated limits and burning the channels that would form the basic circuitry of a civil society.

That circuitry was traditionally Chinese and for that reason, politically intractable and challenging to the Party. Among the new cultural movements was *qigong* – later resurrected as Falun Gong. *Qigong*, at the most basic level, is a set of breathing exercises but is rooted in mystic Buddhist traditions and thus particularly unnerving for the ruling party, aware of how many dynasties of the past have been overthrown by rebel groups led by mystical religious sects. In the late 1980s, *qigong* became something between an evangelical religion and a form of hypnotism. *Qigong* masters filled stadiums and healed the sick and drove people into trances or bouts of paroxysmal joy much as Seventh-day Adventist revivals do in the United States. Offices and factories organised classes in *qigong*. Gurus sold booklets and home-instruction tapes. By the time the Falun Gong protest sprang up in 1999, millions were reading the book of the movement's master, Li Hongzhi, and practising breathing and meditation exercises in public parks in the morning. It was said that several members of the Politburo were disciples. The repression that followed was particularly brutal and engendered China's first coherent opposition movement in exile, with media outlets and Shen Yun performances throughout the world.

Once companies were free to spend a bit of money without prior approval, they began offering perks to employees, like dancing classes and lectures by visitors who had hiked the length of the Great Wall or visited a foreign country. Naturally, entrepreneurs began to offer these services for a fee, and cultural events snowballed.

The arts flourished as they had not in nearly a century. Writers embraced the new "wound literature", expressing the hurts of the Cultural Revolution. Independent painters, formerly limited to propagandistic murals, showed abstract art. Dance parties were held on college campuses. Embassies hosted concerts by the new bard of Chinese anomie Cui Jian, whose hit "Nothing to My Name" struck a chord with young people alienated by the newly materialistic culture. Poets of the new "misty" (*menglongshi*) style travelled to give readings. College students held marches; social unrest spread.

Perhaps the most politically combustible problem was the inflation generated by the investment surges in the late 1980s, because this inflation exacerbated the economic inequalities that had already become so glaring. Inflation rapidly altered the social status of men and women, young and old, and encouraged both corruption and conspicuous consumption – if your money will be worth much less in a year, best to use it now. The media were filled with disapproving images of men who swaggered along the street yelling into suitcase-sized cell phones; mobile phones were a status symbol at the time and were derisively labelled with a Beijing pun that translates to "big brother phones". Wealth had become too conspicuous in the eyes of the elderly political leaders. The privatisation experiment, in their view, had got out of control.

Cultural expression and public assembly, even for breathing exercises, outside the Party's authority was bad enough, but then the public began to have opinions about politics. The dour Mandarins in Beijing tried a few times to curtail the new freedoms, but people resisted and found ways to get around the rules. By 1987, students in Beijing were regularly holding marches from the university district down to the centre of the city – Tiananmen Square – to protest political restrictions.

The protests that engulfed Beijing from mid-April of 1989 until the June 4 massacre by China's military demonstrated the flaws in the political leadership's belief that they could quarantine the Chinese people from foreign trade, foreign investment, private business, and the ideas about individual autonomy that come along with them. Until then, the leaders had clung to the belief that China could reap benefits in income growth – some for regular people, lots for the elite – without having to change internally.

At the end of the decade of opening and reform, the Chinese Communist Party found itself staring down demands to share power.

CHAPTER TWO

THE GILDED AGE
THE SECOND DECADE (1989–98)

The tragic story of the Tiananmen rebellion has been well told outside of China. Less understood are the profound and lasting effects that this failed revolution had on China's political economy over the following decade. The 1989 rebellion persuaded China's top leadership that, if they did not themselves restructure the country's economy, others would, and the Party would be deposed. Fear for their personal well-being was generalised into a fear for the nation. Top leaders persuaded the Chinese people and, perhaps, themselves that a collapse of the Communist Party would mean loosing anarchy upon the world.

The protests occurred during a visit by Mikhail Gorbachev, then president of the Soviet Union, to Beijing, and the subsequent disintegration of the USSR served as a palpable warning of what might be in store for China. The reform coalition around Deng had been tentative and fractious enough; the threat posed by the Tiananmen protests dramatically undermined the loose and experimental nature of his reforms.

Two days before the military attack on civilians in and around Tiananmen Square, according to the book *The Tiananmen Papers*, Deng Xiaoping's inner circle told each other that "capitalists" were plotting to undermine China's progress and playing "power politics". Peng Zhen, the retired mayor of Beijing and revolutionary war hero, added a note that would be echoed over and over and remains a frequently stated justification for Party rule today:

"This month or more of turmoil lets us see how important stability is. Stability is the crucial issue if China's going to shake off poverty and get to the Four Modernisations... We had no real choice about martial law."

For the Party, "stability" has long been a convenient stand-in for "control". These views would shape the policy that emerged in the aftermath of Tiananmen.

The protests had involved virtually every school, factory, and government office in the big cities; if the Communist Party was to remain in charge, it had to marshal a commensurate response. That response had three legs: fear, control, and inducements.

Once the cooperation of the People's Liberation Army had been secured, the fear part was not hard to achieve. Tanks rolled into Beijing, and soldiers shot fleeing protesters. The massacre was kept out of Tiananmen Square, which had attracted too much international attention; the unarmed citizens were shot down or crushed in alleys around the square, as they tried to reach safety. The whole city was locked down: in those days, no one but public officials had telephones at home, and there was only state TV to provide information, so people had to huddle in their apartments, listening to tanks rolling through the streets and wondering if their loved ones had survived.

For about two years after the massacre, China was closed off and "dissidents" were hunted and jailed. An atmosphere of fear engulfed the cities. Anyone who had participated in the marches – and that was nearly everyone – was either disappeared, jailed, demoted, or had a black mark added to their secret personnel file such that neither the participant nor any family member would be eligible to attend university or get a good job. No mention of the protests or repression was permitted in any public forum except using the Party's new narrative: that rioters had attacked patriotic soldiers.

Once the Party felt that its authority had been reestablished via the massacre and arrests, it began to assess the protests. Academics studied the "colour revolutions" of the former Soviet Union and quaked in their boots lest the same calamity should afflict China. Fearing a break-up, the central government embarked on a large effort to tie the provinces more closely to itself. It began a massive campaign of investment in control.

GOOD AS GOLD

Central authorities needed clearer vision into governance nationwide. They embarked on building a series of information technology systems called the "Golden Projects", which were designed to recreate the ancient tools of rulership over an empire that sprawls in both physical and cultural/ linguistic dimensions. While once imperial forces sped across inland waterways and held trade choke points with manpower, now the central government laid out a plan to hold critical information routes on four rigid IP backbones pulled together at just a few domestic data centres like strings of spaghetti tied with a rubber band. Initially, there was one international gateway, the better to sniff, listen to, cut off, and generally control communications. The control, as with all such things in China, was principally directed internally, lest any in the sprawling bureaucracy that manages China have the temerity to challenge Party elders in Beijing, whether ideologically or by stuffing some of the proceeds of economic growth into their own pockets instead of sharing with their superiors.

The first four "golden projects" brought information technologies to customs and tariff collection, intra-government communications systems, and banking. Government communication at the time consisted of an internal courier system that carried documents to each agency, controlling copies by stamping them with legally privileged stamps and numbering the documents, making it illegal, under pain of imprisonment, to share the documents outside of government. Government leaders were provided with private, unvarnished reports on various political issues: for years, more staff of the national news service Xinhua were dedicated to confidential reporting for political leaders than to public news reports. Golden Sea aimed to change the courier system into an electronic network linking China's top government leaders and providing them with live access to data they might need on the economy and the political situation of the country.

Phase two was designed to strengthen tax collection and audits. Phase three had to do with applying the new IT system to the specific needs of ministries: Golden Health, for example, was an information exchange system for hospitals, and Golden Shield was for criminal detection and surveillance. These programmes greatly enhanced the ability of the centre to peer into local economies and capture control. The new panopticon was intended to save China from fracturing under the pressure of the unplanned, unanticipated, and explosive pluralism, diversity, and distribution of resources that blossomed in the first decade of Deng Xiaoping's economic reforms.

The days quickly ended when government officials had to telephone officials of other provinces and ask whether they had implemented a certain law. While, in the early 1990s, a bank branch in Xi'an would require six weeks to clear a cheque from its headquarters in Beijing, as slips of paper had to be mailed back and forth, by the end of the decade, overnight electronic clearing was routine. Round-trip air and train tickets could finally be purchased; the means of managing passengers had been to dole out a given number of paper tickets to each stop on a route, but after the "goldens", tickets were managed electronically.

The final leg of response to the protests involved inducement. Without an ideological vision with which to rally people, the government needed economic growth. That way, the restive students and workers who had joined the protests might focus on economic opportunity and not on social or spiritual dissatisfaction. This clearly worked: the dissidents of Tiananmen flocked docilely to Beijing, where they were followed by hordes of plainclothes police but permitted to sign investment deals. Even Warren Buffett employed one of these former dissidents, Li Lu, whose history of protest provided a burnish of authenticity in the West but who had access to China's leading companies and brokered a deal for Buffett to invest in the Shenzhen auto company BYD.

At this point, nobody wanted to talk about ideology, they wanted to talk about investment and growth, and that appealed greatly to foreign business leaders, who styled themselves as apolitical while relying on China's barely visible controls over inconveniences like wages and unions. To the average person, saying China was communist was just a truism, like the sky is blue or winter is cold. Asking a Chinese official about whether China was implementing socialism was like making a rude digestion noise and would be met with pretended deafness and a clearing of the throat. No one could say whether China's leaders actually believed in a Marxist view of history, though that philosophy was and is still taught in schools.

The leadership was well aware of its power to shape the narrative and summoned all its economic clout to reward those who praised and punish those who criticised the Party. What mattered to the leadership was not the ultimate shape of the economy, nor where they were going, but who got to steer the ship. They deeply believed that the Chinese Communist Party should remain in control and, by the way, reap the benefits of an expanding economy. This meant the Party had to be the architect of social change. Party elder Chen Yun had said that China could tolerate a free economy within the "birdcage" of the socialist structure; the post-Tiananmen government set about designing the cage.

THE GREY ZONE

Zhu Rongji was then the premier. Orphaned by the age of nine, Zhu was smart, humorous, sexy (for a Chinese politician), straight-talking, and arguably more powerful than anyone since Deng in the battered and weakened government structure that had emerged from the Cultural Revolution. Zhu set out to create a new, robust economic architecture that would support and enable growth while maintaining the unassailed political dominance of the Chinese Communist Party. People were released to pursue wealth on their own as long as they stayed out of politics and did not challenge the ruling party.

Zhu almost single-handedly sliced through bureaucratic resistance. Between the reforms of 1993 and 1998, he managed to cut the government bureaucracy in half; privatise housing; sell off about two-thirds of the companies in the state sector; unify the dual currency (before 1994, Chinese were required to use the renminbi and foreigners the foreign exchange certificate); impose a new, nationwide tax system that included a bureaucratically complex value-added tax; bring the larger banks under central government control; get visibility into customs tariff collections nationwide; and capture authority over all major provincial-level appointments. In his spare time, he and others in the Politburo smashed the biggest smuggling ring in history.

The reforms were breathtaking in scope and drew an almost giddy global optimism about China's future. In order to create the new systems, China threw open its doors to academics, corporations, and governments that could offer models and advice. Chinese officials travelled the globe to bring back examples of systems that seemed to work. The nation that had been isolated for three decades and sought nothing from the world outside its tight borders seemed to become an enormous graduate school for open-minded government officials as well as a vacuum for the best practices from every corner of the globe.

The reforms were steered forward through a series of trade-offs designed to ease the state out of direct management of the economy by providing governments at all levels with the benefits of capitalist ownership and control to substitute for the rewards and burdens of socialist managers. But the reformers concentrated economic privilege without symmetrical responsibilities or consequences for failure. Softening the constraints of responsibility and de-risking bold investment were the obvious moves to kick up China's rate of growth to unprecedented levels. The new report-card incentives offered to local officials by the central government drove growth hard, providing the twin inducements of career advancement and opportunity to wring generous measures of family wealth from the bank of public assets. These interests coexisted within the local elites who managed public assets with essentially unchecked authority.

It was by no means an immediate process: since Tiananmen and the political repression that followed, caution had ruled the processes of privatisation greenlighted in the 1980s. Entrepreneurs straddled two political worlds: their investment in state-owned companies might be celebrated as far-sighted but might also be deemed criminal. These new businesses lifted a major burden from the state, but would political figures see the loosening of government controls as too threatening to their own power?

LIBERATING THE ARMY

One of the biggest headaches in Chinese governance has been how to fund the military. At its height in the 1980s, the People's Liberation Army (PLA) operated 20,000 companies, including farms, airlines, coal mines, hotels, and phone networks, and these provided sustenance to hundreds of thousands of military families. Deng wanted the PLA to focus on fighting. He had used his personal capital and his position as chairman of the Central Military Commission to extend deep reforms into the military, professionalising the corps, improving access to new technologies, and demobilising a million uniformed men and women. His government had a stated intention to hive off the businesses that were sapping the energy of the PLA. The programme was accompanied by a large military-to-civilian conversion programme for people, companies, and technologies.

As the military started spinning off businesses, many soldiers continued to operate them while still in uniform. These men and women lived in a grey zone between military and commercial employment, holding on to the security and status of being in the military while earning an income in businesses that had been spun off but remained dependent on the military for contracts and resources.

Shenzhen, a city identified with Deng Xiaoping and managed by his close allies, was a listening post to Hong Kong, then independent and just steps away. As such, the city held communications stations and research and development labs, which easily spun off to become technology companies with reliable military procurement contracts coupled with the exciting growth prospects of the private economy. This was the environment in which, in

1988, ZTE Corp and Huawei were established.

In China, law is merely a statement of normative values; Communist Party policy determines whether people go to jail or are celebrated as heroes. Since then-Party General Secretary Jiang Zemin had no clout with the military, the new entrepreneurs did not trust his government to keep them and their families safe from a turn to the left. Everyone had recent memory of parents, teachers, neighbours, and government officials who had been tortured, imprisoned, and murdered for such "crimes" as selling goods in the free market.

In stepped the war hero and champion of China's opening, Deng Xiaoping. The man who had unleashed capitalism in China made a 1992 southern tour that included Shenzhen and tacitly pushed all these grey experiments into the green. On this tour, he uttered the pithy phase, "To get rich is glorious," which state media reported to have reignited reform momentum. His picture, placed atop the epigram, still adorns a large billboard in Shenzhen. A few months later, the powerful military leader Yang Baibing declared that the military would be the "escort and protector" of China's economic reforms in Shenzhen.

With his southern tour, Deng coalesced a consensus around the continuing bifurcation of the economy into strategic sections that should continue to be controlled by the state and commercial companies, which, like plots of land, individuals could manage under contract. Deng managed to strike a balance between those who would have retracted the economic experiments of the 1980s in favour of recapturing firmer control and those who would have further opened the system and permitted political democratisation.

Deng's southern tour strengthened the reform faction. It

also affirmed for the ruling elite that using capitalist tools within the socialist economy could be extremely lucrative.

The pace of change along with the seeming eagerness to learn from foreign businesses, governments, NGOs, research institutes, and universities won China the most concentrated influx of foreign capital, foreign technology, and foreign practices the world has yet seen, and old investment begat new. The importance of the opportunity to capture and direct these rich flows of capital was not lost upon the Communist Party and its leadership, which conflated personal with public benefit, positioning themselves resolutely as the arbiters and abettors of capital flows as well as the protectors of the domestic industries designated to receive them.

MORE PRIVATISATION

As China focused on growth and attracting capital, it had to create new economic structures with greater autonomy to manage capital. Although the proportion of government ownership of industry dropped each year, public ownership did not so much retreat as regroup into new formats designed to preserve the value of government equity by increasing managerial autonomy.

One such structure was the *chengbao* or "assuming responsibility" system, which permitted government-appointed managers of state-owned companies to retain free cash flow from the companies in exchange for assuming responsibility for operating costs.

Hand in hand with the *chengbao* system came the invention of a private sector. Private companies and "township- and village-owned enterprises" were created provisionally to promote innovation, with the understanding that successful experiments would be taken over by the state if they grew large.

The "group corporation" structure came in in the late 1990s for entities that owned multiple subsidiaries and met certain scale and investment targets. This structure gave profitable state-owned companies a higher degree of control over investment decisions and inter-company financing and was all the rage among state corporations in the 1990s, providing them with far more flexibility to retain capital and deploy it towards new, attractive targets.

The 1990s were a relatively unbridled era for private companies, as the state's regulatory muscle lagged behind the proliferation of corporate entities. Companies were listed on public markets one after the other, generally bearing obligations to government, friends and family, and grandmothers who had been assembled through marketing campaigns to put a bit of money into pre-IPO shares. Once they listed, if the companies found they could not meet ambitious growth targets, many, if not most, ended up tweaking their reports in order to repay the grandmothers and reward local-government sponsors with share appreciation.

This dramatic restructuring was largely in Premier Zhu's hands, and he needed buy-in. Probably only half intentionally, he supported the blindingly fast creation of a political elite to act as stewards of the new economy, and this cohort became cheerleaders for reform. In the era of explosive growth, there was a happy mutuality of personal and private benefits. Naturally, the families of Party leaders themselves were trusted as reliable stewards.

It felt very natural. The system of entrepreneurial skimming by the noble class has the deepest of historical roots in imperial China as well as a long pedigree in other imperial systems, whether Roman, Egyptian, or Russian. In ancient Rome, the equestrian military-commercial class formed corporations that would raise capital from prominent families in Rome and then pre-pay to the emperor a year's worth of taxes prospectively owed by one of the eastern provinces. The equites would then go out to Thrace or Pontus and collect three times what they had paid, distributing the profit among their funders. In China, rulers 2,000 years ago put the country's most valued resources – iron and salt mines – into the hands of a small group of oligarchs entirely beholden to the ruling house. Granting a commercial fief to a trusted associate was an efficient way to receive tax income and control the use of technologies as well as deny enemies access to resources. The emperors, however, did not permit the emergence of power centres that would compete with their own.

Then, as now, in China, a bureaucratic system relied upon a degree of entrepreneurialism among public officials to generate economic returns. Naturally, this led to widespread corruption, but the separation between public assets and private wealth for members of the political class has always been a matter of proportion, not of principle.

Nepotism is practical in the Chinese context of unsecured and poorly defined property rights; the involvement in a business of the son or daughter of a political leader can reduce political risk by staking the political leader in securing the business's interests. Moreover, the ambiguity of the nepotistic connection can be positive, because the connected person is not directly associated with any one organisation or its objectives and personnel. Such an ambiguous elite figure can be a dark-horse negotiator, outside the usual bureaucratic turf battles and yet with the burnish of power.

Private companies surround the state networks like pilot fish, and if one corporate format becomes imperilled, another can just as easily be adopted. This is the mechanism by which bureaucratic socialism managed to grow into a new form of hereditary oligarchy.

RED CAPITALISTS

The hiving off of companies to reliable stewards in the military and in political families began China's Gilded Age, the era in which vast fortunes were made by the new red elite, those connected to the original revolutionary class. As money flowed out of the new corporate structures that were being improvised, the elites did not want it to be funnelled into taxes and social benefits – especially to rural areas, where needs were greatest. To accomplish what amounted to massive social theft, businesses needed technically unaffiliated figures who could move between government and business silos and provide lubrication. The red elite stepped in: they were technically without portfolios but able to access anyone. Their role is not unlike that of private equity managers in the West, but while in the US and Europe, elite universities are the hothouses of the managerial class, in China, accident of birth brings a rich social network and political prestige, and the business elite is a blooded one.

The hot, molten core of the political elite flows through the most influential positions in politics and the state sector. Its members grow up in the same neighbourhoods, go to the same schools, send their children to the same foreign boarding schools and universities, are cared for in the same hospitals, holiday at the same beach spots, join the same clubs. In a system where the government owns or wields decisive influence over all large businesses, political and economic powers are inextricable. The economic players whose interests align most perfectly with those of the political leadership are the sons and daughters of the revolutionary generation. They became investment bankers and corporate leaders, with the personal connections to provide an implicit guarantee of gain for stakeholders in the absence of property rights. These red elite figures themselves relied on a second tier of well-born but lower-profile managers who actually understood business.

Midwife to the emerging elite in tech was Hou Ziqiang, a scientist at the Chinese Academy of Sciences (CAS) who was intimate with but not himself of the first-tier elite – just the type of person who in the early reform period could get things done. Under the state planning system, companies received their capital from the ministries that owned them. Hou, understanding the commercial potential of the internet, chafed at the paltry budgets and lumbering bureaucracy governing emerging technology companies. Hou believed there was greater opportunity to be realised through corporate independence, and he persuaded a couple of the red elite that financing could be separated from management, at least as an experiment.

Grandfatherly, animated, with grey hair and an attitude of barely contained glee, Hou was a supporter of a radically free economy, free flow of information, vigorous competition, and bankruptcy for the uncompetitive. Hou's job was to persuade researchers to leave the womb of the academy and start companies that he hoped would commercialise the technologies CAS had developed.

As a first step, Hou's patrons persuaded the government to let them create a venture-capital fund to uncork the research results of China's scientific institutions and create incentives to commercialise its technologies. That fund, called China Venturetech, was steered by Hou's patron Deng Nan, the mousy second daughter of Deng Xiaoping, along with a daughter of Chen Yun, the Long March veteran and member of Mao Zedong's inner circle.

In the end, new technologies made up little of Venturetech's portfolio; there were not enough money-making projects to support. Quickly, Venturetech became a lender to industries from retailing to chemicals as well as a speculator on the stock market. Venturetech drowned in debt and was closed in 1998 as part of a nationwide clean-up of the financial-services sector.

Hou's most powerful ally in tech was the restive scion of President Jiang Zemin's family, Jiang Mianheng, a moon-faced engineer with his father's pained, daffy smile. After earning a PhD at Drexel University in the US, he returned to Shanghai to found one of the most influential private equity funds in the country, and soon he was a captain of industry.

Dubbed "Mr Ten Percent" by detractors, Jiang chaired or owned significant stakes in a major telecommunications carrier, an airline, and at least a half dozen other companies in media, internet, broadband, automotive coatings, and semiconductors. Jiang Mianheng founded the first quasi-independent telecom company, called China Netcom. He formed a bridge in the tech industries to Taiwan, joining with Winston Wong, the philandering son of Formosa Plastics chairman Wang Yung-ching who had been exiled to the mainland after a stormy affair. Wong and Jiang partnered in the biggest information-technologies venture the mainland had yet hosted, Grace Semiconductor, and a family of related companies. Bill Gates joined with Jiang in research and development efforts in China, as did many US technology firms.

Premier Zhu's own son was a key figure in the emerging blooded elite. When China created its first private investment bank, the China International Capital Corp (CICC), as a joint venture with Morgan Stanley, Zhu Rongji's son, Levin Zhu, was assigned to head it. CICC become a critical and obligatory participant in the wholesale restructuring of Chinese state industry to create asset packages that cosmetically resembled international corporations and therefore could be carried to Hong Kong for market flotation. Cutting three telecommunications companies out of the old Ministry of Posts and Telecommunications in order to float China Telecom, China Mobile, and eventually China Unicom, was the first ambitious step.

In finance, Rong Yiren, a close friend of Deng's, was given the charter to break the Bank of China's monopoly over hard-currency banking, founding the China International Trust and Investment Corp (Citic). Rong was scion of a wealthy industrialist family in Shanghai that owned textiles and flour companies before the revolution. He was the greatest of China's "red capitalists", the group who helped in the nationalisation of their properties after the 1949 revolution and joined the new government. The Chinese government was then filled with men like Deng Xiaoping, who tended to hold meetings with their trouser legs rolled to the knee and a cigarette dangling from the lips. Rong, with his full head of white hair and elegant frame, cut just the figure of international sophistication that China needed.

In his later capacity as vice-president, Rong met many visiting foreign dignitaries. Rong's son Larry Yung (who had adopted a Cantonese transliteration of the family name) took over the Citic affiliate Citic Pacific and became one of the wealthiest men in China. He stepped down following a corruption scandal but formed a new business that helped make his three children, treated as royalty in Hong Kong, extremely wealthy.

After Rong, Citic's paterfamilias, retired, Wang Jun, his right-hand man and the son of another Long Marcher, forged alliances with companies bearing a military stamp – from Great Wall Broadband Network (headed by his younger brother) to Poly Technologies (whose CEO was Deng Xiaoping's son-in-law). Along with the Wangs, the children of Deng ended up overseeing the formation of an independent military-industrial complex that created better technologies and made more profit than the armaments factories captive to the Ministry of Defense ever had.

In electric power, the children of former Premier Li Peng helped drive a new breed of independent power producers. In telecommunications manufacturing, the old government monopoly broke up after the former Minister of Posts and Telecommunications and his wife agreed to spin out and sell off factories the ministry had operated. They took generous personal stakes in them. These equipment companies, retrograde in their management practices and still reeking of the state economy, became the berths of the most ambitious of China's Gilded Age capitalists.

In a sense, Deng's moderate group of allies became the new old-money class in China. Deng ally Marshal Ye Jianying, though he died in 1986, lived long enough to ensure that the ultra-wealthy Ye family to this day dominates a sprawling empire in banking and finance, travel, property, and weapons. The sons of early Party hero Bo Yibo (one of whom, Bo Xilai, later attempted to lead a coup) grew wealthy in finance and tourism. The sons of revolutionary elder Wang Zhen came to dominate military procurement. Ironically, apart from Mao's own progeny – there remains only a grandson, who appears to be intellectually impaired – there is no member of the post-Mao elite generation who is simply middle class.

By the turn of the new century, children of the top leaders controlled virtually every major part of the Chinese economy, the cross-provincial behemoths in sectors like telecoms, petrochemicals, and finance. But they left the little things, like convenience stores and small factories, to the little people.

RED ELITE

The most perfect expression of the Gilded Age's alignment of interests is the private equity fund, through which the red elite can command state resources and convey them into companies of interest, accessing future cash flows for themselves while also watching out for state interests. The US$1 billion Boyu Capital, a private equity company founded by Jiang Zemin's grandson Alvin, aggregated partners who formed a flexible and conveniently unseen governing council through private equity funds. The elite founders of private equity funds in China have included Jiang Mianheng, Levin Zhu, Premier Wen Jiabao's son Winston Wen, and many more. In fact, there may be no Politburo member, current or past, who lacks close family ties to private equity.

The great private equity groups have been critical to

building the underground cistern that connects private businesses one to another and allows for a mutual-support network of cross shareholdings, contracts, and joint investments. Private equities have also forged links among companies internationally. IDG, a fund created by a US publishing group, was among the earliest and largest and became ubiquitous in Chinese tech and media investing. Sequoia China overtook IDG, as that company's publishing empire withered. Among the native groups, Jack Ma's Yunfeng became perhaps most incestuous of all, with ownership and board seats spread among investees such as Alibaba, Sina, Sohu, NetEase, and Giant Interactive.

The process was in many ways productive. In using influence to create special concessions in the state-run economy, this red elite spurred innovation and competition for the sclerotic national leviathans that had been created to monopolise banking, trade, telecoms, and manufacturing. Each fissure in the top-down, command-control system ultimately created an entrée for others. As the economic system cracked and money started to drift free, enormous social change ensued. By pursuing their self-interest, China's superelites became agents of growth, innovation, competition, and massive privatisation of the Chinese economy. The children of the Communist revolution dismantled communism – temporarily. The goal was to enable economic growth but never to let go completely.

Unlike the Russian oligarchs, the leading Chinese families are never permitted to grow so rich and powerful as to threaten the primacy of the Communist Party. They must promote government agendas, even when those agendas make for money-losing business propositions. In exchange, the Chinese super elite are permitted lucrative concessions that allow them to acquire overseas real estate, foreign educations for their children, and the ability to pass on company equity stakes and management positions to the next generation. Wealth grew to unprecedented levels.

The step-by-step dismantling of the Chinese socialist system was a thrilling event to witness. It was also key to capturing surging foreign-investment flows and the initial public offerings that fuelled the Chinese economy's phenomenal growth in the early part of this century. While everyday people were generally feeling optimistic about their improving prospects, in less than one generation, a class of the super wealthy emerged. As long as there was growth for all, nobody really minded. They would remark on the changes, shaking their heads. In most people's living memory, a penny ice cream bar was a luxury: when frozen, chocolate-covered ice cream cones emerged costing 60 cents renminbi – about eight cents US at the exchange rate of the time – people were scandalised by the inflation. Yet soon the elite class was buying dainty holiday treats from Häagen-Dazs for US$150 a box, not to mention driving imported sports cars and travelling to the Maldives for scuba-diving holidays.

The Chinese Communist Party understood that there was a gun held to its head: as long as the economy was humming and providing lots of opportunity, inequality would not matter. If growth slowed or stopped, it would be another story. China's leaders had placed the ambitious economic restructuring into trusted hands, but in doing so, they created a degree of elite wealth and privilege beyond anything the world had seen. The Chinese people shrugged, because things were getting better for everyone. But when a global economic crisis rolled through emerging markets in 1997, Chinese leaders quaked in their boots: they feared that the export machine driving the economy forward would stall.

THE CRISIS DEEPENS

China's Gilded Age capitalists had the penchant for luxury similar to that of America's nineteenth-century railroad barons. China's millionaires and, now, billionaires enjoy a level of conspicuous consumption matched only by the most decadent dynasties of the past. Chinese corporate chieftains became the biggest buyers in the world for private jets and superyachts. They became fixtures at luxury boutiques in Paris and London and New York.

The levels of visible corruption became operatic. One example was when the powerful former Politburo member Zhou Yongkang, who acted as head of China's security services, was arrested on corruption charges, investigators claimed they had seized liquid assets worth about US$14 billion. The system was rocked by the Lai Changxing scandal, in which one company in Fujian Province was reported to have evaded US$3.9 billion in taxes over a period of four years. A vice-governor of Anhui Province was convicted of stealing US$4 billion. Corruption had been an integral part of the system for decades, but it had moved from packs of cigarettes and bottles of liquor in the 1970s to hundreds of thousands of dollars in the 1980s and now, routinely, billions. That degree of wealth is not so much corruption in a form recognisable anywhere else but a major national enterprise, one that has as its core competent political power.

The numbers associated with these political identities suggest not so much personal graft as the control of large and complex businesses. China's army and government bureaucracies not only sell positions but have developed lending rackets to finance the ever-rising prices of what are lucrative positions. These systems in turn create an entrenched expectation and indeed need to continue relying on graft, as new aspirants arrive in office encumbered by debt. As expectations throughout the bureaucracy rise, there is more pressure on the system to deliver growth. As soon as growth is hampered, it becomes genuinely dangerous to the political powers that be. The only practical solution is to narrow the base of support and therefore the quantity of officials who need to be fed and cared for.

Watching the emerging market crisis of the mid-1990s, Chinese leaders worried about exports. They had no idea that they would soon confront a decidedly capitalist phenomenon: the bursting of an investment bubble. The 1998 collapse of the new investment schemes formed in the 1980s presented an even more terrifying scenario than the possibility of export decline. Chinese leaders feared that the new elite would lose their money and grow hostile to the reform faction.

A banking crisis would be felt by everyone, would undermine the image of competence projected by the Party, and could not therefore be contemplated. So, when an investment company called the Guangdong International Trust and Investment Corp (Gitic) collapsed, it sparked a chain reaction that led to a massive bank recapitalisation.

Gitic was one of the many investment vehicles set up by local governments in the early days of reform. Because Gitic was government-owned, its investors, who included foreigners, believed its debts were guaranteed. Premier Zhu felt he had to break that moral hazard and keep locals from thieving too many assets. In January 1999, Zhu forced the company to declare bankruptcy. After that implicit guarantee was removed, the scale of failures was breathtaking and quickly lapped upon the shores of the big state banks. The resulting bailout cost China up to 40 per cent of its 2002 GDP. Ultimately, it was more of a rollover than a rescue. The immediate economic pain was fairly light, but the structural damage to the economy was deep.

The historic bank recapitalisation took four years to complete, from 1998 to 2002, and opened a pipeline of cash. As a first step in the bailout, China's government coralled bad debts into new institutions. In 1999, the government established four asset management companies (AMCs), each as a sort of evil twin to one of the Big Four banks: they were receptacles for the bad loans their doppelgänger banks needed to get rid of. The government then printed new money to replace the unpaid debt and handed it to the AMCs. Each AMC was instructed to take the cash it got from the Ministry of Finance and use it to buy bad loans from its mirror bank at 100 per cent of the value of the dead debt. If, for example, a textiles factory had borrowed US$1 million from the Industrial and Commercial Bank of China (ICBC) then went bust, the ICBC would get US$1 million from its associated AMC, China Huarong, and China Huarong would get a claim on the bankrupt factory.

The first tranche of funding wasn't enough, and the banks got iterative injections of money. The government had to push deposit rates well below lending rates so that depositors were giving the banks free money, and that financial repression has to be counted as part of the bailout. Between the bank bailout and the export boom that followed China's accession to the World Trade Organization (WTO), money just poured in, and investment capital lay thick on the ground.

The people at the top of the pyramid could see problems were emerging, but they stuck their fingers in their ears and hummed: money, when it's coming in, feels good, and no one has an incentive to reduce the flow. The tip of the pyramid included foreign investors and a few lucky Chinese entrepreneurs, as well, of course, as the red elite, who went to Davos and wrote op-eds about protecting the reforms and generally became so-called thought leaders on China.

Hosing cash on the economy to forestall a banking crisis launched a decade of euphoric growth, during which there was an explosion of wealth unparalleled until the global financial crisis. Dark clouds were gathering, but the international class, which supported the narrative of the Communist Party, ignored them. There would be time enough to find an umbrella.

CHAPTER THREE

THE GO-GO YEARS
THE THIRD DECADE (1999–2008)

As China entered the new millennium, a coarse capitalist energy entered its bloodstream and infected the brain stem with the dizzying idea that great wealth was just around the corner. When structural change was creating opportunity, everyone seemed optimistic about their own future and the future of their country, and they didn't mind seeing some people get disproportionately rich. But after the banking crisis and subsequent bailout, structural change slowed, and money accelerated. Those who found themselves in the path of the flood felt they had to grab handfuls of cash while they could. If the 1980s and 1990s generated money for bootstrapping entrepreneurs, the turn of the century rained drug lord-type quick money into the hands of anyone ruthless enough to reach out and take it. Coal barons bought stables of racehorses. Local officials drove Ferraris. Mid-ranking police bought apartments for younger, well-dressed mistresses. Whole cities developed reputations as the homes of *ernai* or second wives. China's economy became a sort of golem, eating more and more capital and growing at a breakneck rate into a shape no one had foreseen. No longer did people aspire to a quiet apartment, a steady job, and a family; everyone was going for the brass ring: a home in New York or London or Sydney, a private jet, an IPO, and a US green card.

And it was tantalisingly possible. Money came sluicing into the economy; getting rich seemed easy. Any expat or Chinese "returnee" entrepreneur who failed to make a fortune in business during that era had to be either dumb or very unlucky. It was as if all China were Silicon Valley, and everyone was a software engineer. Foreign company factotums sent from headquarters to run an ice cream shop or an engine factory in China felt like masters of the universe. Chinese returnee entrepreneurs could do no wrong. Freebooting young foreigners would arrive in China with a job at a law firm or a consultancy or audit firm, and a year or two later raise funds to start an online travel company or a manufacturer of pool tables or a genomics institute, then – win or lose – they would walk away with a chunk of cash. That elevator to riches made everyone an evangelist for the promise of the Chinese economy.

Since money flowed freely, the new entrepreneurs tolerated the loss of the openness of the 1980s. The freedom of the teahouses, private concerts, art exhibits, and samizdat publications was replaced by money-fuelled nightclubs and private strip shows. Gone were the quaint *kunqu* opera houses and the Shaanxi storytellers. Now Beijing had a bar that offered girl group performances in weirdly tight harmonies to visiting North Korean bigwigs; the waitresses wore their Kim Jong-il buttons inside their clothes because, they said in broken Chinese, it would be disrespectful to wear his picture openly in a bar. There was a nightclub called Chocolate for the Russian diaspora where the bouncer packed heat, patrons drank Georgian champagne, and dancers wearing tight leather shorts and pasties writhed in cages. There were whole districts where nothing opened until midnight, and nothing really happened before two. This go-go era was China's version of leisure suits, cocaine, and Studio 54, a time when driving a Volkswagen instead of a Jaguar made you look like a chump, when newly minted millionaires booked mile-long sections of the Great Wall for private parties and hired Sherpas to carry baskets of champagne on treks in Tibet. It was a general bacchanalia driven by uncertainty about when it all might end and the unspoken knowledge of the newly wealthy that they had not really earned their stash.

This decade was also the era of foreign success. The international world thought China was shaking off its socialist past and would soon lead the world both economically and politically. That led to both anxiety about the relative decline of the West and optimism about China's limitless growth. Before China entered the WTO in 2001, the US railed against the Chinese export engine and the way Chinese products were undercutting American goods. Then for a few years, Americans and Europeans become obsessed with China's "indigenous innovation" drive, believing that China would surpass all the technological achievements of the West. Everyone, including the Chinese leadership, believed that China would share power in a triumphantly bipolar world in the twenty-first century, if not supplant the United States.

One bubble succeeded another as money from the bank bailout rolled from a tech bubble into property. China went on a valuation tear. An investment of US$40,000 this year in a private company might be sold to a venture capitalist next year for US$400,000, then might glean US$4 million the following year in an IPO. Anyone who figured out how to surf the valuation wave got rich.

There were three classes of wealth aspirants. First were foreign nationals assigned to head the Chinese branches of big corporations like GM, BASF, British American Tobacco, Cigna, and Yum!. The most ordinary manager from a tomato canning factory in the US could command base pay twice his or her US compensation, plus free housing, a driver, private-school tuition for kids, and "help" with taxes. It was not unusual for a mid-tier manager at a big corporation to fetch US$500,000 in annual compensation – the same person who might make US$150,000 back at home.

Foreign corporations were convinced that China was a deeply mysterious place where only the native born could figure out the bureaucratic relationships needed to succeed. Foreign businesspeople also felt they needed visibly to pay respect to all-powerful government leaders who held the keys to the economy. As a consequence, one after another multinationals began to form Chinese holding companies and appoint China-born executives as chair. These executives generally came from the second group of China gold diggers: the returnees, called "sea turtles", were Chinese people educated overseas who had probably worked for a financial institution or a tech company before returning to China to start a new business. Chinese governments at every level fawned over this group by offering income-tax reductions, special rates on mortgages, and, of course, high salaries if they took government jobs. The Party worked with various associations to encourage these sea turtles to purloin technology from their foreign employers before returning, but even without intellectual property in hand, returnees found local governments, foreign companies in China, and local financiers highly receptive and happy to employ them. Some of the famous returnee companies included AsiaInfo, Suntech, UTStarcom – many, if not most, have since collapsed.

The third group consisted of people you might call "in-pats", expatriates who had not been sent to China by a big corporation but had chosen to go to seek their fortunes. These people generally learned the language, lived in Chinese neighbourhoods, and prided themselves on understanding local politics and culture. They started boutique consultancies, founded trading companies and outsourced-research companies, teamed up with a Chinese national, and tried to IPO the company or at least get acquired by someone bigger. Many made their fortunes, but these people, understanding China but not themselves Chinese, were eventually targeted by a vengeful bureaucracy for detention and expulsion, since they knew, or pretended to know, too much.

But while a lot of money was deployed by entrepreneurs, even more fell into government hands. Government-owned companies plunged into share-trading, real estate, grandiose industrial plans, new types of financial institutions, and, always, golf courses. The enthusiasm for investing in all sorts of businesses created an era of spectacular booms and busts.

The breakneck growth of this decade brought with

it environmental abuse at an unprecedented level. This densely populated country has for centuries been ruled by emperors whose interest was in exploitation rather than sustainability. China's natural environment has been one victim. But the drive after Mao into a coarse form of state capitalism wholly focused on windfall profits has created environmental devastation that blanketed China's cities with smog, destroyed farmland, and poisoned the majority of its rivers. The contamination exposes the common view that Chinese leaders are long-term planners: the entire focus of the reform period has been on generating economic growth at any cost to the environment, and if hundreds of children must comb through the shells of discarded computers to retrieve cadmium from batteries, or if a few people die from cyanide that has leaked into a river from a gold mine, so be it.

The property craze accelerated the environmental destruction, while wasting energy and resources: all of that iron ore dug out of the ground in Australia and shipped to China, all the coal burned, all the cement manufactured, have greatly accelerated the planet's problems with greenhouse gases.

GOING GLOBAL

One of the consequences of the money fountain was a big boost in industrial subsidies. The key targets were exports and technologies that would replace imports, because these would help the government to aggregate hard currency. In reality, the subsidies undermined the industries' competitiveness by focusing companies on the wrong targets.

Take mobile handsets. In the late 1990s, domestic companies were making just a few plastic handsets for simple mobile phones. The foreign companies Motorola and Nokia dominated the handset market with a massive export share. Government leaders set their sights on overtaking these leading lights and set forth an aggressive plan of support for domestic handset makers who could export. The electronics ministry proclaimed that it would support the emergence of eight national champions via R&D supports.

In terms of volume, it worked. By 2006, domestic brands were exporting almost a half billion phones. But in the rush to achieve volume, Chinese manufacturers fell off the technology curve. Core technology for handsets had to be imported from France, South Korea, and Taiwan, with kits from these countries generally including chips imported from other nations. China's No. 1 handset player, Bird, purchased its handset kits from Sewon and Telson, South Korean companies, and from the French company Sagem. Fully assembled sets accounted for around 50 per cent of total Bird sales; Bird branded the imported sets and marketed them domestically and overseas, making Bird China's top handset vendor in terms of sales volume. Most Chinese handset makers assembled semi knock-down kits.

In the early 2000s, the software that runs handset functions became a more important portion of the value proposition. So did chipsets, LCD screens, and eventually the form factor – Apple's sleek iPhones became a fashion statement. China's domestic players had been too busy achieving volume to focus on developing technology, and that affected their margins. Now, the national-champion handset brands of the time – Konka, Panda, Hisense, Southtec, Kejian, CEC – have disappeared.

Subsidies to the steel industry were more focused on papering over company failures than on developing champions. The steel industry consists of state-owned companies that cannot be allowed to die. Steel is the very core of the socialist industrial system, and as such, it has attracted the greatest subsidies. Bloated with investment capital, when steel mills started to falter, local government forced them into mergers and acquisitions that, according to the Chinese Iron and Steel Association, led them down a "road to poverty". The association estimated that its 87 member companies had a total debt in 2012 of ¥3 trillion, or roughly US$5 billion per company.

Another cash-gorged bubble industry was solar. Start-ups like Suntech, LDK, and Trina Solar listed on US markets in rapid succession, and US investors told one another about the brilliant returnee founders who were pulling China up the technology stack. It was not enough to manufacture the lower-tech final-stage assembly portions of the solar value chain: the goal was to go vertical and build world-class polysilicon plants. Each level of government supported the construction of such plants with gifted land, cheap loans, subsidised coal, and preferential infrastructure. Foreign investors responded by buying the companies' equity and debt. LDK was the company that proved to some that China could do it right: they hired a top international engineering firm and head-hunted talent from the leading polysilicon companies around the world. Photos were posted weekly showing the progress of construction of their world-class plant. The world celebrated China's mounting another step on the innovation ladder and gasped with admiration at the scale of the capacity build-out.

In the end, LDK tried too hard to impress. When the company's state-of-the-art polysilicon plant ran into problems, LDK built a small, dirty plant nearby. Impressive scale and the reach for a wide swath of the value chain resulted in over-commitment. After losing 25 cents for every dollar of product it sold, LDK had no hope of paying US$4.8 billion in liabilities and ended up delisting in disgrace from the New York Stock Exchange.

Suntech Power was the earliest of China's solar companies to list in New York and became the largest of all. Suntech benefited from a rich origin myth concerning the brilliance of its founder, a Chinese returnee from Australia. Suntech also ended in bankruptcy. Baoding Tianwei Baobian, parent of the celebrated, New York-listed Yingli Solar, was another company that built a polysilicon plant, only to default on a loan.

One of the sadder aspects of China's "green energy" explosion has been the way in which Western nations have exported their environmental problems to China. To capture technology and market share, Chinese companies skipped over clean technologies like closed-loop processing in polysilicon manufacturing and blithely ignored the need to recycle chemicals like the toxic silicon tetrachloride used to make this basic material, instead dumping it in fields. "The fruit that grows here is poisonous," commented a farmer outside an LDK facility back in 2010. "We never eat it; we sell it in the cities."

Even skipping over costly but life-saving recycling technologies, China's solar companies failed to thrive. The default events seemed always to be laced with accusations of fraud, misrepresenting assets, misrepresenting market demand and buyer commitments, failing to disclose material if not major changes in operations or financial status to investors, and the transfer of assets to the mainland to protect them from creditors who had a legal right to them.

The ease of raising capital based on an exciting story was just too tempting, and market bubbles inevitably involve fraud.

THE CHINA HUSTLE

Some entrepreneurs took advantage of the freewheeling attitudes and the mystery that investors attached to China. The boom years began the era of the "China Hustle", when public markets, recently discovered, were treated like giant piñatas for enterprising entrepreneurs.

International stock markets highly valued Chinese concept IPOs, which used scientific-sounding language, uncheckable metrics, and references to a vast but completely unmeasured and unmeasurable market. There was THT Heat Transfer Technology, Inc., which manufactured "plate heat exchangers and various related products"; Tianyin Pharmaceutical, which made "stimulated egg powder" for veterinary applications; Shiner International, which made "biaxially oriented polypropylene (BOPP) tobacco film"; and three different companies making organic fertiliser. Companies in traditional Chinese medicine were especially popular, since their medicines generally conveyed incomprehensible benefits like "improving qi". There were also the usual bubble companies, like Dog, Where, a pet travel service, and Sweet Pea Square Dance, which taught dance via online classes.

Some truly imaginative business ideas got to market in the heady days of endless stimulus and larger-than-life numbers. Kuangchi Science, listed in Hong Kong, made materials for cloaking devices on spaceships and said it built apparatuses for space tourism. China Agritech, formerly listed on NASDAQ, reported that it had developed "fertiliser nanotechnology". China Medical Technologies in its prospectus described "ECLIA" technologies without explaining the acronym. "Our ECLIA system, which consists of reagent kits and an ECLIA analyser, is an IVD system based on enhanced chemiluminescence immunoassay technology." Mazu Alliance, once listed on the Australian exchange, was dedicated to the worship of a goddess called Mazu who supposedly had a cult in Fujian Province. Yuhe International raised chickens for a single day starting from when the eggs hatched. Yuhe would then sell "day-old broilers" to chicken farms. Before it delisted, Yuhe reported that it had capacity to hatch more than 3 million chicks.

An advantage of very obscure products is that there is no comparable company to provide a reality check on margins or market size. China Cord Blood was among the first companies to offer storage of umbilical cord blood. China Biotics sold "live microbial food supplements". HQ Sustainable Maritime offered beauty products made from tilapia.

Then there were the bigger and more plausible companies. Before Longtop Financial, no one had heard of "core banking platforms", but Longtop, before its chairman admitted that the company had been lying about its US$1 billion in cash, persuaded investors that this was a very real and very valuable technology. Giant Interactive, the gaming company, told investors that they could not possibly understand the free-spending ways of customers in "low-tier cities". Some of the high-value players of Giant MMORPGs residing in these rustic areas, they reported, spent as much as US$1 million just to buy virtual goods in the game. "You don't understand," the investor relations staff would say. "Players in third-tier cities are just crazy." Giant, now delisted, is a gaming company in more ways than one.

For the builders of temples, promoters of pilgrimages, and gaming companies raking in mountains of profit from third-tier city gamers, the blizzard of unaudited statistics with questionable relevance to the business could be blinding – but still compelling for owners of shares in companies like Alibaba and Tencent. E-commerce companies, for example, tout their gross merchandise value (GMV), a vaguely bounded measure of online sales and other transactions originally intended to impress. Alibaba destroyed its own credibility with a GMV that bloated to astronomical levels as a product of huge annual growth rates and started gamely qualifying it until the company decided it should no longer report GMV except on the "Singles Day Festival" – itself an invention. But, like the billion customers that used to be invoked by any Western company justifying an investment in China, GMV was there as a symbol, to impress with sheer, incomprehensible size and growth rates.

One after another, Chinese companies were exposed as frauds and delisted from US markets, generally keeping the windfalls they had gained from the IPO but losing the trust of investors. The "China Hustle" era did much to support a view in the West that any Chinese company was a congenital cheat.

PROPERTY BUBBLE

The mother of all boom-bust cycles was in property. The re-capitalisation of the banks was the ultimate source of the asset bubble in housing, but a private real estate market was the necessary precondition.

In the 1980s, urban employees, assigned to work in organisations after graduating from school, waited years to be assigned an apartment and spent endless hours currying favour with the officials who allocated housing; a popular pun was supposed to be the expected answer when asked about your housing allocation: "we're considering", which in Chinese is a near homophone for "cigarettes and liquor", the bribes of choice in the pre-reform period. Factories were like small cities: they provided apartments, kindergartens, hairdressers, restaurants, and their top executives could grant employees permission to marry or send them to jail. Some people spent their whole lives within the compounds and gave their children names like Little Electricity (for a girl born in a power plant) or Weather (for a boy born in the metrological bureau compound).

In the late 1990s, this began to change. State-owned enterprises shook off the responsibility of providing housing, along with other social services, to their employees. Between 1998 and 2003, the urban housing that all work organisations rented to their employees for a pittance was sold to the occupants. The units were sold cheaply, but any income for the enterprises was a positive, and meanwhile, they shucked off the cost of maintenance. Everybody won: state-owned enterprises became profitable for the first time ever, and households were enriched by a large transfer of assets.

Privatisation generated enormous demand for housing, as, after a holding period, the new owners could sell at a mark-up and buy new, nicer housing. Then, worried about disappearing farmland, in 2001 the State Council restricted the sale of land, crimping supply amid the swelling of demand. Prices soared.

The Chinese property dream started as an antidote to the tax reform of the 1990s, which beggared local governments. Before 1994, central and local governments shared tax revenue based on formulas hacked out in an annual negotiation. Everyone was tired of the negotiations and the games governments played, and they struck a deal under which the central government established its own offices to collect nearly all taxes directly, after which they promised to remit a generous portion back to the localities.

Over time, the central portion of revenues grew, while the local portion stagnated. This was exacerbated by corporate reforms – once companies no longer had to turn over all their cash to their supervising government agencies, there were many methods and plenty of incentive to demonstrate low profits. The local share of tax revenue fell from 78 per cent in 1993 to 45 per cent in 2002. Local governments were also barred from borrowing or from running deficits. They imposed a blinding array of fees, but these were not enough to patch over the missing tax revenue.

The bigger problem was that the term "local" was not clearly defined: China has five levels of government, and, as taxes trickled down through the levels, the last two or three were left with very little. Yet these were the governments tasked with paying for everything of importance – from schools to hospitals, water systems, roads, power plants, and welfare programmes. The lowest-level governments were also the least well-equipped to handle these tasks in terms of the educational level of their officials, their experience in managing budgets, and the resources they could command.

The solution? The local government financing vehicle, Governments, meanwhile, had access to land to use as collateral. Governments also can generally be relied upon not to disappear. To marry these two sets of advantages, governments formed companies – the LGFVs. As companies, they can borrow and collateralise land handed to them by governments. As government-owned entities, they enjoy quasi-sovereign status. LGFVs hold an implicit guarantee against default. Over the two decades following the invention of LGFVs, the banks nearly wet themselves in their eagerness to lend to these entities.

China now has more than 10,000 LGFVs. They operate urban infrastructure, like subway systems, water, and gas utilities, and build and operate real estate developments. Because their government owners can mandate relocation of government offices, schools, and other facilities, the relevant LGFV can guarantee occupancy in any residential development – if people don't want to move, the government cuts off bus service from the preferred residential district to the new area. To fill up new schools, the government might dynamite the old ones. One local government in Inner Mongolia not only blew up schools that students stubbornly refused to leave but, when its GDP lagged as a consequence of unsold property, it blew up the empty towers and built new ones. Because of these government powers, there is probably no city in China that lacks a new district of government offices and residential towers.

Cashed-up from LGFV borrowing, governments promised their people a better way of life: they would build new roads, subways, and pedestrian malls, and the town would become a city. In China, "city" is a bureaucratic designation determined by a certain density of population and certain types of infrastructure. When a bureaucrat becomes an official of a city rather than a town or county, he or she gets higher pay, better benefits, and more clout.

Everyone wants the status of urbanisation. The principal engine of urbanisation is what you might call urbanisation *in situ*, meaning changing the designation of a particular area from rural to urban, reclassifying all the residents as city dwellers.

A key propellant for the property boom has been the urban-rural divide enforced by the policy of household residence or *hukou*. Rural and urban populations have traditionally been and still are subject to different legal regimes, different access to state resources, and ultimately very different levels of importance in government policy. That creates strong incentives for rural people – about two-thirds of the population – to obtain urban residential status.

China's management of *hukou*, implemented at the very start of the People's Republic in 1949, implicitly assumes that land provides all reliable subsistence and that rural populations, who have access rights to communal land, do not require the resources of a government. Classically Marxist in its approach to urban versus rural areas, the Chinese Communist Party concerns itself with managing the means of production and leaving agriculture to local village councils. The countryside, in the Chinese system, is supposed to be self-sufficient.

The *hukou* system expresses a legal apartheid that has led to partitioned systems of social welfare. An intricate architecture of bureaucratic rules specifies what sorts of schools, hospitals, parks, and other facilities should be provided for rural residents and for urban residents, driving a complex range of incentives in today's economy. A Chinese citizen with a household registration designated "rural" may move just a few metres away, but if the new area has an urban designation, then that resident will have access to better schools, better hospitals, more parks, a better social insurance system, and a better chance for his or her children to get into university. The lure of such "urbanisation" lies behind the mass acquiescence in the orgy of housing construction by local governments.

For those governments, it meant that clearing farmland – getting residents to move so that governments could build high-density complexes – was a winning deal. Basically, the government buys 10 acres of farmland that would normally accommodate 40 families. Once the land had been cleared, and new roads and other infrastructure built, the land can be designated "residential" instead of "agricultural", dramatically raising the price per square metre that a developer will have to pay. And because local officials are compensating farmers with new apartments, they can claim in their business plans that a certain percentage of units were pre-sold. They sell the farmland to a developer who builds high-rises on a half-acre. The families move into the apartments and, presto, with this higher density, they are now "urban". The former farmers are assigned "urban" jobs like tending the boiler in the new buildings or operating the elevators.

To understand how odd this is, consider a typical example: a locality where everyone grows corn. To upgrade the price of land and sell apartments, government officials need to entice people to sell their rights to till the land and use the money to buy an apartment. But the market for a luxury high-rise development in the middle of cornfields may be sluggish, and local farmers are probably worried that if they give up the corn, they won't have an income. To solve that problem, officials reserve a small portion of the money they earn from selling land to pay the salaries of cleaners and elevator operators in the new high-rises for a couple of years.

In building towers on what used to be farmland, the government can claim higher population density and use that to apply for "urban" status. With that status in hand, they can go to local farmers with a great deal: trade your acre of land for a 90-square-metre apartment in a modern high-rise. Change your *hukou* to urban and, presto, your children can attend better schools, you can access better healthcare, and you can give up the back-breaking work of cultivating corn and instead push a broom around the apartment building for a monthly salary. Since the new jobs are fundamentally uneconomical and are funded as part of the development package, the guaranteed salary eventually comes to an end.

But in spite of the fine print, who wouldn't accept the deal? Everybody wins: the locality sells land, builds new infrastructure with the proceeds, and writes lucrative contracts with nearby friends who express their thanks with generous kickbacks. The former farmers get cash windfalls, nice new apartments, and they no longer have to do back-breaking work in the cornfields. Local elite-owned construction and material companies rake in windfall profits. The developer makes a tidy sum.

All the elements were present for a national construction project that would make the Great Wall look like a Lego set. Less successful was the actual economy. A town that two years earlier grew lemons may not have been wealthy, but it at least produced lemons. After "urbanisation", there were high-rises, a bunch of former farmers pushing brooms around, and no lemons. Since a steel mill and a construction company were busy building the high-rises, the devastation to the area was not immediately evident. What is clear is that, when there are fewer lemon groves every year, you have to build another high rise to stand in for that productivity you've lost. The high-rises have to be financed. Nothing in China can default, so this just keeps going on and on until you have jaw-dropping debt and ghost cities of a scale never seen before.

Commercial housing became a new class of asset, a means of storing value, like big jewellery. It's been a good investment for most people: even after declines post-2021, housing prices in China have reliably grown by nearly 8 per cent annually over two decades – at least to the extent that we have numbers for them. The Shanghai stock market, with much greater volatility, has returned 2.3 per cent a year on average since 2000. Deposit interest rates at banks have hovered below 2 per cent annually, spiking to 4 per cent in 2007. Various investment schemes have periodically offered much higher returns but with high risk, and the risk-free types of investments return something close to the bank deposit rate. Add to this the fact that the average Chinese person doesn't trust the banks. No wonder Chinese people have been speculating in real estate. The Chinese have used housing the way Americans use mutual funds – as a reliable growth tool, something to leave to one's children, with the added bonus that, if something happens to the market value of an apartment, you can always live in it.

The new formula for housing construction spread nationwide. A few years into the current century, only the poorest Chinese actually needed housing, but they were priced out of the market, and the wealthiest bought multiple units. Already by 2003, the vacancy rate for commercial residential property was recorded as 61 per cent in the eastern part of the country – people were holding property for resale. From 2009, the statistic was no longer made available.

According to a survey undertaken in 2012 at the behest of the central bank, 85 per cent of urban and an amazing 93 per cent of rural families owned at least one dwelling, far higher than the average US ownership level, which was 65 per cent despite strong government supports for ownership. The survey found that 15 per cent of households owned more than one unit. A decade later, the accumulation of new housing units was mostly by the wealthy, who already owned several homes. Some cities have been reported to have an average home ownership per family of more than five units. The average amount of residential space per person also rose dramatically, from 6 square metres per urban resident in 1985 to 26 in 2005 and 49 square metres in 2020. Since the average household consists of more than three people, a typical urban family had around 150 square metres to live in by 2020.

The whole Chinese economy is surfing on property speculation, and values of residential real estate, albeit in vast oversupply, have risen higher year after year, often in double digits. The rare exceptions when property prices flatline are always linked to slowed growth in the money supply, not to bedrock measures like employment rates or household wealth. What sustains high residential property prices, which still exceed those in most of the fanciest cities in the world, is not an excess of demand over supply. It is rather a unique combination of Chinese features, including the state ownership of land and the local government allocation of it, local government dependence on rising land values, local government involvement in building materials and construction, and local controls over postable land values and sale prices. Taken together, these interventions have jacked up property prices to levels far, far beyond what any natural market would support.

Pricing declines for housing are in no one's interest – not even in the interest of individuals and not even of the poor, since there is no actual shortage of housing in China, and rents are relatively low compared with housing prices. Of course, the poorer classes are inadequately housed, but it is migrant workers who face the biggest problem finding affordable housing, and that problem has more to do with the *hukou* system that keeps them from settling in cities and from selling dwellings in their hometowns than it does with the housing market. Few migrant workers lack housing in their native places.

REPLICA WONDERS

One remarkable aspect of sudden wealth is the yearning to give it historical legitimacy. The Chinese version of the dream is an aspiration, a vision not of how its buyers hope to live but of how they imagine wealthy people must want to live.

There are wonders of this world that have to be seen personally to be comprehended, for which photos cannot do justice, that words can never fully describe. Recognised among these are the Grand Canyon, the Dead Sea, the Eiffel Tower, the terracotta warriors, and the Great Wall of China. More recently are China's grandiose replica cities. There are at least three little Hong Kongs; a couple of Manhattans; a Little Paris in Anhui; a Florence with Venetian canals and gondolas; a detailed replica of a mansard castle with its own vineyard outside Beijing; a Red Square, complete with a model Kremlin, in Hebei.

There's Little Manhattan in Tianjin, a city that has always been a poor stepsister to Beijing, a failed port economy on the cuff of the national capital, suffering from urban blight with an entrenched underclass. At 11,758 square kilometres, China's Baltimore is larger than Lebanon and has roughly the same population, which justifies some spending, but perhaps not the amount it gets: Tianjin periodically gets about US$2 billion to play with.

In its Little Manhattan, Tianjin dug its own "Hudson River"; built a new World Trade Center, empty but with gleaming towers all around it; opened an imitation Javits Center; and, incongruously, built replicas of the Sydney Opera House and the world's largest mall, the Mall of America (which is far away from Manhattan, in Minnesota). Little Manhattan has pitched itself as a new financial centre for northeast China, steadfastly ignoring what people in the original Manhattan know well: that a city is an organic entity that grows over centuries and is dependent on the dynamics of diverse populations and fertile cultures; it is not just a collection of buildings.

Casting a jealous eye over Little Manhattan, officials of other zones in Tianjin vied to create new, self-contained cities in the broad swaths of farmland, ramshackle housing, and warehouse space around the city's core that have until recently been occupied by shipping companies, oil depots, and the low-rise homes of longshoremen. In the wild, unoccupied zone west of Tianjin city lies the Xiqing District, which was revived by Goldin Properties, a Hong Kong developer. In Xiqing, Goldin created a perfect model of a polo club, with 270 imported horses trained by Argentine polo champions and a luxury hotel with rooms fitted out with mirror-embedded televisions and Nespresso machines.

No detail was ignored in this mad, empty pleasure palace and field of dreams. Another district has built terminals for cruise liners and an artificial sandy beach in hopes that tourists will come to sunbathe, although they will have to do that in the shadow of oil terminals. At least two of the zones are building waterfronts with docks for pleasure boats that are to carry tourists on new Florentine canals.

Cities throughout China joined the rush to replicate the real landmarks that people actually wanted to visit. In a small city in Inner Mongolia that borders Russia stands a Russian Orthodox church that is forbidden to offer services but exists as a backdrop for photographs. The same city, Manzhouli, also has a large "Matryoshka Park" with larger-than-life models of nesting dolls to represent every country. The doll for the US is painted to represent Walt Disney. Manzhouli also boasts a model Kremlin and a Russian circus, although there are few, if any, performances.

When all the new construction began, residents were optimistic: they would cycle past the empty complexes and imagine that their cities would soon bustle with commercial activity. But towards the end of the decade, doubt crept in. The dark, looming towers of every city in China started to look like spooky monuments to the go-go decade that was coming to an end.

In the boom years, the Chinese cities couldn't stop building these mirage-like complexes, because it would force them to confront their total, abject failure. The Ozymandian zones would be comical if it were not for the tragedy that the people's money had been so wasted, and wasted while China's masses have been left sorely wanting for the most basic social infrastructure. Health and educational standards in China have regressed and trail those of such developing countries as Algeria and Thailand. And because admitting the failure is so hard, the local governments and even the cleaners and the taxi drivers continue to shore up the hallucinatory vision of futuristic cities filled with skilled, wealthy people enjoying happy lives of consumerism and leisure.

Perhaps the jewel in the crown of the manic build-out was the 2008 Beijing Olympics. No public works project in China's history could have rivalled the Olympic preparations for scale and intricacy of social engineering. Not only were new stadiums built but factories were moved out of the cities to reduce pollution. Rain was induced before each visit of the Olympic Committee to impress the foreigners with clear skies. Special farms, roads, and rail carriages were created and dedicated to Olympic supplies. Police were issued arrest quotas to keep the streets free of undesirables. All buildings facing public roads were required to be repainted in one of five designated colours. Beijing's taxi fleet was replaced wholesale, and taxi drivers, newly drilled in English, had to wear a uniform.

The most obscure and unrelated events throughout the country were coloured by the Olympics preparations and measured by whether they met the national standards for the image the government intended to project. New control systems were put in place on internet and telephone communications. Spending on domestic security was hugely increased. When a large milk company found that its aggressive addition of melamine to infant formula, designed to increase the measured protein content, had led to babies' deaths around the nation, the company and the government together agreed to suppress the information lest the Games be marred. Factories were closed and steel mills commanded to suspend production to clean the air for the Olympics month. Hotels, which had invested massively in new facilities in preparation for the influx of foreign visitors, were informed at the last minute that visas would be strictly controlled. Residents of the city were encouraged to stay at home, and new driving restrictions were put in place. It was said that China spent US$1 billion on the opening ceremony, which was choreographed by China's renowned and quasi-official film director, Zhang Yimou. The government preferred that the Games be played to an empty city, all the better to maintain complete control over the images projected from within. Not even North Korea has ever undertaken a programme requiring the same degree of social coordination and control.

The historic increase in the power of China's central government that had begun after Tiananmen made possible the frenzied construction drive – a Marshall Plan for China but much, much bigger. That money sent the Chinese people into a frenzy of speculative investment. Every farmer, every college student, every housemaid had capital in some scheme or another. It was Bernie Madoff times 10. Since the bank bailout that ended in 2002, China had chosen capital over the public. As political leaders doubled down, in came the era of the billionaire.

But in the early months of 2008, China's economic heart began to beat more slowly. Because the pending Olympics had driven the capital city into fevered preparations, the rumblings of the coming earthquake were mostly ignored. The crisis that began in late 2008 became a turning point in China as momentous as those of Deng Xiaoping's historic opening in 1979 and the protests of 1989.

Increasingly, it became evident that the replica cities and the stage-set Olympic Games were creations of a frayed

DNA, one that produces dysplastic growths that serve no purpose for the body as a whole and in fact represent a danger to its survival. They are overgrowth of a development model well past its prime. The replica-wonders bear unimpeachable witness to the last throes of a growth model that must change to something slower and more sustainable. But whatever plans had been made to make China's growth more sustainable were knocked out of their guardrails by the global financial crisis. All of a sudden, concern about the health of the nation was tossed aside, and China grew laser-focused on avoiding financial collapse.

CHAPTER FOUR

THE CRISIS
THE FOURTH DECADE (2009–18)

There is an old story in China about a train whose last car is on fire and has to keep accelerating to stop the fire from moving forward. In 2008–9, the fire was a smouldering pile of unpayable loans that China had ignored for a decade. Political leaders had demanded top-line growth that could be achieved only by stoking the economy's engine with new debt, and the faster the economic train could move, the more it could blow back the licking flames. But Chinese acceleration had been fuelled by the global economy. One day everything went belly-up.

On 15 September 2008, the US investment bank Lehman Brothers filed for bankruptcy. People watched on TV as hundreds of the former kings of commerce left the building in New York in a walk of shame carrying cardboard boxes full of their belongings. Lehman had been the cynosure of the banking industry, viewed as the most perfect of banks, and now stood at the centre of a maelstrom. In the simplest terms, unfettered crony capitalism had created a monster.

Watching the storm from behind the walls of the Zhongnanhai compound at the heart of Beijing, Chinese political leaders quaked in their tasselled loafers. How could they have ignored the long and ignominious history of financial crises in capitalist systems? And it got worse: a month after the Lehman collapse, stock markets across the world plunged. Banks looked like they might fail, and hundreds of millions of people would lose their savings. Cratering international demand would mean less cash crossing the border into China. At the height of the crisis, in October 2008, Chinese leaders must have gone to bed imagining angry bank depositors rushing towards Tiananmen Gate with cleavers.

With the global financial crisis, Chinese policymakers saw that the train was going slow and might be consumed. They had to find a way to create financing within China. They decided to roll down the security grilles at the borders, seal off the economy, and make sure no angry mobs would come for blood. Planners argued that the economy had grown excessively dependent on exports, and China needed to return to self-reliance. The nation would create its own demand and generate its own growth. To make this happen, the government printed money and threw it in fistfuls at local governments. What was already a property feast became a feeding frenzy.

The first-order need was to reassure both the Chinese people and the world that, whatever happened in the West,

China would be fine. The State Council approved an investment plan of ¥4 trillion, a number intended more to impress and reassure than to represent any real intention. Next, authorities had to get the money moving. The central government called on local governments urgently to submit wish lists for their favourite projects (within two weeks) for review. Central authorities laid out general areas for investment and top-level amounts they would invest. Provinces provided a lengthy array of shovel-ready projects that totalled around ¥25 trillion, since there was no downside to overshooting. The locals were happy to hand over lists whether or not they were practical – Christmas came early in 2008.

The stimulus plan China assembled in early November gave local governments a political mandate to spend money. Counties, cities, and provinces went searching for plausible excuses. Mostly, they dusted off blueprints they'd already prepared for the next Five-Year Plan, focusing on two top-line targets: heavy infrastructure and growth substitution via industrial investment and property. The plans strongly favoured rail and subways, gas pipelines, highways, and power plants. By mid-December, the central government approved the first tranche of investment.

Because the construction was self-justifying, governments had only the vaguest plans for how these facilities might be used. Many projects were built for reasons other than market demand and without market research or projections. For example, Tianjin built three terminals for luxury cruise liners even though none docked at the city. Yunnan Province laid out a 150-kilometre canal just to fill a fanciful moat around a new hotel. Cities built new airports with no flights, schools without students, libraries with no books. A city in the dunes of the Gobi Desert dug out a reservoir and filled it with water so that imaginary visitors could sail boats.

Projects have, naturally, been subject to regular cost overruns. The Beijing-Tianjin Express Railway shows how desire for speed overruled common sense. The original plan was for a 200-kilometre-per-hour line. That was upgraded to 300 kilometres per hour for a 75 per cent higher budget. The boost theoretically would shorten the ride by 10 minutes, but since the acceleration-deceleration cycle is 26.2 kilometres, compared with 8.9 kilometres for a 200-kilometre-per-hour train, the advantage of this extra speed for the 120-kilometre trip is next to nothing. The cost per minute gained was about ¥900 million.

Many airports were built, even though 70 per cent of China's airports were failing to cover their own costs – a good gauge of demand. Lots of existing airports were expanded. There was the Guizhou Province Qiannan County Libo Airport, located in a national park. The airport reportedly had a throughput of 151 passengers in 2009. Zhangbei airport in Hebei Province got a ¥100 million facelift, even though it was not approved for commercial flights; the plan was to have helicopters fly the one-hour Zhangbei-to-Beijing route to boost tourism. But Zhangbei is one of the poorest places in the country and does not attract a lot of tourists.

There were highways and bridges to nowhere. Already, by 2012, China had three times the length of highways per unit of GDP as the EU, twice that of the United States, and eight times that of Japan. The cash-fuelled growth carried China far from the promise of the early reform and opening, as a whole new class of speculators got rich. But in the short term, it assuaged fears of crisis, and that's all anyone had time for in 2008–9.

INDUSTRIAL BUBBLE

Alongside infrastructure came industrial plans, designed to create a new path to growth for the economy, which would be freed from depending on export processing. In the first six months of 2009, the bureaucracy put out in rapid succession plans for investing in ten "strategic" industries, including autos, steel, shipbuilding, machinery, light industry, textiles, and telecoms. These were largely dusted-off plans from the 1990s but contained industrial and planning targets dear to the hearts of many public officials. The plans included funding to reach production targets, R&D support, various subsidies, and tax incentives for localising the components base in order to reduce imports.

In telecoms, China built out its fibre network by about 30 per cent annually, spending over ¥50 billion per year in 2009–10. The telecom carriers vacuumed up new subscribers, and money trickled down to components and chipset players, who benefited from the increasing smartphone and 3G handset penetration. Network integrators such as ZTE got new business. In machinery, there was funding for companies making excavators, shovels, and bulldozers, with particular emphasis on developing hydraulic technologies that were seen as lacking.

The funding was so extravagant that money had to be pushed out to engorged local government and company accounts, then rules made to force them not to simply hold the cash. Loans were abundantly available. Banks hired call centres to offer unsecured loans to consumers. Traders stuffed their warehouses with over 100 million tons of steel (or said they did) to meet the formality of collateral rules so that asset-light service companies could take advantage of the cheap loans.

One of the marquee plans was for China's steel industry, which had already been targeted for mergers and acquisitions of upstream assets by the grand steel plan of a decade earlier. Since steel is almost entirely state-owned, it's easy for the government to meddle in the industry. Huge steel plants had been required to move out of the big cities to clean up the air for urban residents. The programme designated new "industrial bases" where steel mills, mines, and plants to make pipes and steel wire would cluster. Capital Steel had moved as part of a plan to build a steel base in Hebei Province's Caofeidian port, complete with iron and coal mines and loading facilities for barges to ship iron ore. The city of Caofeidian invested close to ¥1 trillion to build out its facilities, while Beijing also shelled out to support Capital Steel's move out of the city.

Bureaucrats complained about the difficulty of getting companies to use the funds allocated for things like R&D; investment opportunities in real estate were much more remunerative. The growth-substitution plan easily morphed into property development. For example, at the time of its move, Capital Steel was already in decline, losing ¥2 billion per year amid growing new liabilities, so its new hometown did not really benefit from steelmaking, but Caofeidian and the surrounding Tangshan municipality did realise a real estate bubble. There were dozens of empty towers, eerily vacant parks, schools without students. The bubble reached a scale that makes Detroit look like an Alpine village. The move, the subsidies, and the build-out of housing that would notionally be needed for the steel production base showed that real estate development could plug in for industrial growth.

This happened in part because so much capital investment was entrusted to local governments, but the localities are ill-equipped to build up particular industries. The investment calculus for companies is complex: they may need a certain density of consumers, access to a supply chain, or certain types of logistics. Companies, not governments, are best situated to decide. Governments tend to think in terms of sunk costs – what assets do they have and how can they be used? Governments accommodate industrial plans dictated by the central government by building real estate projects that appear to fit: "bases" for steel production, coal logistics parks, innovation parks, warehousing and logistics centres for e-commerce. To create a sense of viability, governments get local companies to set up offices in the new parks so that they can run their revenues through the new branches and generate tax revenues for the zone to triumphantly report; no matter that the city proper lost those same revenues.

GHOST CITIES

There is no better example than Shiyan, a small city more than 1,000 kilometres west of Shanghai, of how Chinese governments used real estate to fulfil growth-substitution aspirations, where policy-mandated credit for investment, relocation, and development substituted for declining industrial output, lagging household consumption, and stagnant productivity growth. It worked, but for a very short time.

Shiyan is the dark heart of China, in western Hubei Province, a forested mountain redoubt where Bigfoot is supposed to roam. It is the legendary birthplace of China's Yellow Emperor and, historically, the origin of Chinese shamanism, the culture of the ancient Chu state. Once a remote and uncivilised geography where exiled high court officials were sent to spend their twilight years, it is in the far western corner of this province that Mao Zedong decided to seed China's automotive industry.

Paranoia and political cunning drove Mao's Third Line policy to hide strategic industries deep in the mountains. Mao's model for war came from World War II. He imagined invaders would come on foot from the coast or else look for targets by eye from low-flying planes. In making his Third Line plan, he studied the Soviet Union's shift of its defence industries east of the Ural Mountains. In 1965, China began mandating that facilities doing R&D or building tanks, semiconductors, weapons, and communications move to remote locations. Deep in the belly of China's forest and mountains, Mao thought, foreign invaders would never find these facilities. In the end, China built about 600 factories and research institutes in its heart of darkness. Not coincidentally, the effort required large new investment that benefited Mao's chosen cohort rather than the vested interests at existing facilities in more developed areas.

China's auto industry grew out of this plan. Mao himself loved automobiles but thought them frivolous for the Chinese people, and promoted bicycles for civilians but motorised vehicles for the military. Chongqing, for example, a hilly city near the Yangtze's surging Three Gorges, hosted a large manufacturer of tanks. In the effort to become more commercial, the company licensed the Japanese Alto passenger car. First Automobile Works (FAW), in the thick forests of Jilin where nomadic northern tribes once roamed, originally made the Liberation truck for the army. FAW transitioned in 1958 into cars with its Red Flag luxury sedans for senior Party officials, producing a few dozen each year. Even the champion of private carmakers, BYD, got into the business by acquiring a military factory in the ancient western capital of Xi'an.

Shiyan is among the many cities that benefited from the Third Line. It went from a community of a few hundred subsistence farmers in the Qinba Mountains to a region of 3.4 million with 500,000 in the city core, hosting the immense Dongfeng Motor, Volvo, and Peugeot plants, as well as a suite of auto parts companies. The city became a Dongfeng company town.

But Shiyan is a highly inefficient place for auto manufacturers, lying as it does far from logistics hubs and from steel and electronics industries. Planting much of China's auto industry there in effect imposed a tax on the whole industry. In 2004, Dongfeng decided to pick up its headquarters and move to Wuhan. At that point, Dongfeng had 124,000 employees in Shiyan and owned 57 per cent of the city's industrial assets. Press outlets in 2004 estimated that Wuhan would gain ¥30 billion per year in tax revenues from Dongfeng's move – so Shiyan would lose just as much. That's why, when Dongfeng decided it had to leave the mountains, it committed ¥4 billion in new investment to Shiyan, mostly for real estate projects. The company's real estate arm began major residential projects in the city.

Shiyan's subsequent property boom saw average prices triple in five years, from a bit more than ¥2,000 per square metre in 2009 to nearly ¥6,000 in 2012 even as the city was in industrial decline. With autos accounting for nearly 70 per cent of the local industrial economy and Dongfeng Motor the vast majority of that, the move to Wuhan harmed Shiyan. But the pick-up in construction and property sales made up for the sharp shrinkage in auto-related industries. The local economy diversified into construction, including steel and cement production. Local tax revenues were sustained by the sale of land. The local political structure mobilised to attract companies like Burberry, Swatch, and Starbucks, which built stores in the promising new malls.

It didn't work for long. Shiyan was singled out by China's real estate information network Soufun as the home of one of China's "ghost cities", with massive new and unoccupied inventory. As in so many Chinese cities, a whole district was given over to empty towers. Palm-lined luxury complexes, completely desolate, are a jarring sight in the middle of this dusty and mountainous industrial city.

Beihai on the Tonkin Gulf near Vietnam provides another example. This dark, trading port – where rats leap across the wharves and mouldy, Western-style buildings neglected for a century line the pedestrian shopping streets – is a military zone with a small population and modest economy. In China, zones occupied by the military, with its fat budgets and incentives for graft, often attract extravagant investment. In Beihai, government investment sucked the city into a speculative maelstrom. Clusters of villas were built near the ocean for the imagined new leisured class. The developers soon abandoned both the villas and the debts, but the construction, for a time, boosted the local economy. Filled with empty luxury developments, Beihai saw some of the nation's fastest GDP and industrial production growth after the 2008–9 stimulus. The sale of luxury cars, liquor, and wristwatches soared. And yet Beihai continued to look like a poor city: grimy, heavily dependent on small-scale fishing and pearl cultivation, the highly coveted position of dockworkers, with visible social problems like drugs and prostitution, and idle people on the streets.

Every town seeking a boost to growth took advantage of the boundless appetite to invest in real estate. The tourist town of Lijiang in the southern province of Yunnan, near Thailand, built apartments for at least 350,000 people the town hoped might move there. Once completed, the empty units stretched for an unbroken 15 kilometres along a deserted highway. The city of Manzhouli, near Siberia, tries to pitch its deep forests as an ideal place for city dwellers' holidays. Manzhouli built summer lodges to attract vacationers, but without success – the region is far enough from city centres that flying to South Korea or Japan is just as economical and much more diverting. One thing these developments tended to miss is that people holidaying in remote parts of China like rustic holiday homes, cabins on a lake or in the woods, not mansions with grand marble pillars and chandeliers in the foyer. But localities, competing for buyers, never dare to skimp on fixtures. Expensive fixtures are also a convenient channel for kickbacks – who knows what a fountain with nymphs carved of stone ought to cost?

Cities found that grand events could marry infrastructure investment with a push to property values. Cities eagerly followed the Olympics playbook that had garnered so much praise for China in 2008. In 2009, Beijing organised a celebration of the nation's sixtieth anniversary on a scale of delusional grandeur that would have made the Egyptian pharaohs blush. In 2010, Shanghai hosted a World Expo. Also in 2010, Guangzhou held the Asian Games, and in 2011, Shenzhen held games called the Universiade. Each city competed to offer a spectacle even grander than the last. If the events failed to attract crowds, cities commanded companies to purchase tickets and bus students in from neighbouring provinces to swell the audiences. Analysts from the investment banks were beside themselves with enthusiasm for the growth these spectacles seemed to represent.

The financial crisis stimulus meant printing a bumper crop of cash, and there was too much to digest domestically. The surfeit had to be exported. China stepped up its Going Out programme of overseas investment and renamed it the Belt and Road – a programme of soft lending to support acquisition of energy and mineral resources overseas, and the development of infrastructure to help carry those resources back to China.

ADVANCE THE STATE

China had been consuming 40 per cent of global commodities since the housing boom began and wanted to secure access to iron ore, crude oil, trace minerals, and more. The goal was to buy up mines and oilfields overseas and then to build sea lanes and rail lines to bring the commodities to China's refineries and steel mills. The lending programme was particularly liberal: Venezuela received US$42 billion in soft loans from China for oil infrastructure – not including complementary loans to Chinese companies building infrastructure in Venezuela. Chinese automakers got subsidies to realise their ambition to increase exports and sell into more-developed markets. There were big deals to acquire mines in Australia and Sierra Leone, chemicals in Canada, oilfields in Angola, oil-processing plants in the United States. In 2012, 52 per cent of China's overseas investment was in energy and 12 per cent in minerals.

Some of the purpose of these investments was to capture

contracts for new infrastructure projects that would support the export of Chinese construction machinery and of personnel. The Belt and Road created a mechanism for Chinese banks to invest in Chinese projects that happened to take place offshore. The Belt and Road is fundamentally an extension of China's domestic economy, where high-level national targets require accelerating levels of commitment. The macro figures are in themselves the goal, and the specific deals do not really matter that much. As a result, investment targets tend to be guided by the short-term advantage of connected parties. Why, for example, in 2013 did the chairman of a government-owned telecom company, with no visible experience, financing, or motive, announce he would raise US\$40 billion to dig a canal through Nicaragua, the upper thigh of Central America? Some saw long-term strategic vision in the plan. But another, more cynical view observed that Xinwei, the telecom company making the investment, believed it could capture government financing for a notional contract in Nicaragua associated with the "canal" without ever having to dig. One should expect enormous kickbacks all around.

After China's real estate development fantasy began to evaporate, the Belt and Road also began to unravel. Whether the domestic real estate bubble or the international Belt and Road, surplus capital flowing from China's monetary printing presses had created this investment bacchanalia. As domestic developers started facing down bankruptcy, so did foreign borrowers. Big recipients of loans such as Venezuela and Ecuador went into distress. Facing a wave of defaults, panicked Chinese lenders called in loans to dozens of countries, including major debtors Kenya and Pakistan. Many countries who borrowed from China,

Sri Lanka for example, have had to choose between default and unemployment, reduced salaries for civil servants and electricity cuts.

By making loans, banks actually create money, and money creation in 2008–9 was beyond anything the world had seen before. The fiscal spending on the stimulus was dwarfed by the rush of credit through China's banks. In five short years, Chinese banks added assets – loans – worth the entire value of the US banking system, which had taken 150 years to create in a country with a much larger economy.

The spending on capital programmes generated massive overflow into gambling, luxury goods, and really everything else. Bottles of average-quality blended white spirits that cost tens of renminbi to make were priced at ¥10,000 or even ¥100,000. There were successive investment bubbles in cigarettes, tea, garlic, certain breeds of dogs, art, broad beans – just about anything. Private banks were found secured by inventories of liquor, because the value of these inventories could do nothing but rise.

Much of the investment world's enthusiasm for China has been driven by the idea of a persistently large middle class in formation. The problem is that the people in China who spend money at middle- or high-income levels generally have very low incomes. An American with an income of US$50,000 may be much more careful about spending than a Chinese who earns a quarter of that amount. Lack of· sustainable income is a function of the political economy: the state tends to push risk onto private players and individuals, whose income streams are highly volatile. Consequently, consumption in China is highly pro-cyclical.

High spending in China has generally derived from windfall gains, largely in property. China invests about 45 per cent of its GDP each year – an extraordinarily high figure. A good deal of that money is inefficiently used and ricochets back to individuals via commissions, kickbacks, land sales, appreciation of stocks and other assets, and so on.

The surge in money has had many consequences. One is the recapture of the economy by the state. As money was pushed out on orders from Beijing, much of it threatened to be diverted, whether into alternative, speculative investments or simply into the personal accounts of connected people. Beijing required reliable stewards for its investment capital. Law and regulation remain feeble tools under single-party rule: it's better to own a piece of a company. Beijing's trusted lieutenants, it turned out, are those entities in which the central government has appointment power, access to economic information, a say in investment decisions, and a right to profit streams: state-owned companies. Equity shares became the only practical means of oversight and control. So the investment programme of 2009–10 became synonymous with the "advance of the state, retreat of the private sector".

The "advance of the state" as a national policy has been around since 2000, when China's government started fretting about whether market mechanisms were distorting the supply of coal and electric power. The idea of re-nationalising big parts of the economy caught fire in 2008–12, after the stimulus package created supports for state-owned enterprises while letting private enterprises fall by the wayside.

The coal industry demonstrates the logic behind "advance of the state". The campaign to capture equity in the mines for national-level state enterprises had as its driving goal Beijing's perceived need to control energy prices.

After persistent, deadly mining accidents, the government mandated safety equipment, but mine owners said they could not afford it, given controlled prices for coal. Planners had to let coal prices rise, and next, the power producers clamoured for hikes in the prices of electricity. Bureaucrats at the national planning commission would complain about all the distressed phone calls, first from a mine owner, then a power producer then the State Grid, which had to buy power from the power producer, or from a railway operator that wanted to charge more for shipping coal from mine to power plant. Price controls were seen as a given – the pesky owners were the problem.

The central government decided to do away with the micromanagement and control the value chain directly. Provincial and private owners of mines were offered buyouts by the big national companies, and if they refused, there might be an accident in the mine that would force months of closure. In 2010, the National Development and Reform Commission confirmed the success of its policy by issuing the notice "Accelerating Coal Mine Consolidation" giving broad direction for the next phase.

For central authorities, the re-nationalisation of the coal industry was a policy success. But it represented a solution to only half of the problem. With "consolidation", the state could achieve a much higher degree of control over pricing and supply of coal, but energy policy remained fused with industrial policy. There was no body that could balance the interests of power producers against coal miners, reward higher efficiency, and reduce environmental degradation. That has led to all sorts of policy swings: coal shortages were met with panicked imports, which in turn led to rushed approvals of new mines and higher emissions.

THE BILLIONAIRE FACTORY

Another side effect of the stimulus, as in the rest of the world, was the manufacture of billionaires even as China's "soft" infrastructure, including education and health, lagged. Instead, cash flowed into the pockets of the ultra-wealthy via swelling property, stock, and other asset markets.

The flow of money in China since the global financial crisis has generated fortunes counted in the tens of billions. Beijing now has more billionaires than any other city on Earth, even New York, according to the BBC. Back in 2012, Bloomberg reported that the 70 wealthiest members of China's National People's Congress had in a single year added to their fortunes more than the entire net wealth of the 535 members of the US Congress – not a group known for its poverty. Li Hejun, founder of the solar company Hanergy, was a debutante in 2014 but saw his fortune rise by a factor of seven, to US$26 billion, in 2015. Tencent's Pony Ma was not poor before the 2008 crisis – his net worth was reported at US$1.6 billion – but in 2022, it was estimated at US$48 billion. William Ding Lei, founder of NetEase, went from US$1.1 billion in 2006 to US$25.5 billion in 2022. Colin Huang, a founder of Pinduoduo, was worth US$27 billion in 2022. In 2023, the eighth wealthiest person in the world was someone no one has heard of: Zhong Shanshan, whose company Nongfu Spring sells bottled water. He was worth about US$67 billion. Jack Ma's personal worth grew by roughly a factor of 50 in the decade after 2008.

To an extent, the IT revolution enabled this aggregation of capital. Technology makes it possible for money to fly over borders. It enables portions of a production process to be unstrung and each – the software enabling an elevator, for example, or the accounting system used to manage a complex company – to attract its own valuation. Then there are the margins. Tech companies are uniquely able to amass capital because of the virtual nature of their product. If a company sells you a desk, it must purchase the wood, the nails, the metal brackets, the finish to make the desk, and no matter how awesome the desks, the manufacturer will be limited by the physical constraints of production. Not so a Google, a Facebook, a Tencent, or an Alibaba: after breaking even on, say, search, the marginal cost of additional advertising revenue to Google is zero, and the company can keep creating more and more Google ads into the millions, billions, trillions. After the stimulus period, the free money shot out of the combined central banks' howitzers clung to the tech companies as hair to a lint roller.

Corporate practices developed in the West made it easy for individuals to capture a big chunk of that money. China followed the US and Europe in the 1990s by enabling corporate management teams to control cash flows and direct the lion's share of company wealth to themselves. As executives managed to hold onto money generated by their companies, they found they had powerful incentives to argue for low taxes and government support for their firms. Corporate capture of political systems has occurred in different ways in different countries, but overall, the swelling of money has coincided with the undermining of regulatory regimes and acted as a prime mover of that change. Since the financial crisis, wealthy individuals have had enormous influence not only on economic systems but on legal ones – think about Jack Ma's impact on China's banking system with Alipay. It is little wonder that the post-2009 era saw political leaders in China trying to clip the wings of private billionaires from Jack Ma at Alibaba to the leaders of Dalian Wanda, Anbang, and the Tomorrow Group.

A natural symbiosis has arisen between great individual fortunes and political autocracy. Political centralisation enables focused deployment of capital and other resources. Highly centralised governments can deliver regulatory favours in return for benefits like bribes, campaign donations, or promises of investment. They can also deploy capital on complementary targets by, say, creating an investment programme in semiconductor manufacturers fabs and requiring those factories to buy equipment from certain companies.

These phenomena of rapid wealth aggregation, globalisation, and cosiness between the hyper-wealthy and autocrats have been revealed, with compelling clarity, to be a fundamental threat to democracies. The cost of dictatorship is always born by the poorest citizens, from whom escalating extractions are required to maintain patronage and power at the top. That inevitably requires a loss of political power for the majority, even in systems where top leaders are ostensibly chosen by a voting majority.

After the financial crisis, the world generally believed that strongly centralised power had saved everyone from running over a cliff. Whether the Chinese people, foreign investors, or the Chinese leadership itself, everyone seemed to agree that China's state dirigisme and colossal capital investment had saved the globe from an even more dire crisis.

But the financial crisis had deep and lasting effects on China's political system. If, in 1979, the Chinese people had seen the failures of socialism, now they confronted the failures of capitalism. Some of the shock was felt in the mass relocation to apartments in suburban areas, meaning families were estranged from social context. Some of it has flowed simply from the visible devastation of the countryside and the looming empty towers. Economic change has also embittered many. The end of productivity gains and of income growth to households means that many, many people have taken on mortgages and car loans that put them under intense strain and leave them with little discretionary income. The system of residential permits remains in place, while there are fewer opportunities to make money with seasonal labour. Lack of social mobility is more politically toxic than inequality of wealth.

THE NEW EMPEROR

To listen to public accounts, Xi Jinping emerged like Zeus from a thunderhead, wreathed in godlike power and dubbed by the international press as China's "new Mao" and "new emperor". His ascendance was intended to mark a historical shift from a poor, humble, supplicating nation into a self-styled aggressive global power intending to use its military and economic might to reshape international institutions and activities according to its own myths of paternalism, non-interference, authoritarian control of public discourse, and one-way capital flows directed to China.

Xi and his cohort have promulgated the China Dream catechism that espouses a powerful international image for China, the plan to make the renminbi a global currency, and the Belt and Road plan to re-establish what are essentially tribute relationships in Southeast Asia and emerging economies around the world. Creeping territorial claims in the South China Sea, assertiveness over Hong Kong, and the projection of China's authoritarian principles internationally through its cybersecurity regime are the sticks in the carrot-stick expansion equation.

The agenda of national "rejuvenation" that Xi declared as his goal requires that official history be rewritten to show that the Party is the culmination of a proud historical tradition. The very first thing Xi did as Party leader in 2012 was to stage-manage an exhibition at the National Museum of China on Tiananmen Square in Beijing, which recast the history of the Communist Party as a native Chinese masterwork that owes more to Confucius than to Marx. The exhibit also positioned the relationship with Taiwan as one of understanding brotherhood rather than antagonism.

Xi has had to manage the narrowing of the Party's political base, reassuring core supporters that they will be favoured in an increasingly risky constellation of power. Elites may imperil their lives and livelihoods by supporting an ultimately losing faction, and when governing factions become less popular, they tend to secure elite support by claiming continuity in a long line. That is arguably key to why systems become quasi-hereditary: Xi is son of Xi Zhongxun, a revolutionary cadre who is credited alongside Deng with having founded the city of Shenzhen. After all, China has had very few peaceful transitions of power. Deng Xiaoping walked from prison into Zhongnanhai by way of a coup. Jiang Zemin took over only after Deng's originally designated successor had been deposed and imprisoned. Hu Jintao undertook purges of Jiang allies, with limited success, since Xi supporters complained that the Jiang faction limited their ability to manoeuvre even when the old man himself was in his nineties and seemed very feeble. Peril surrounds succession events in the Chinese system. The promise of continuity contained in bloodlines helps assuage the anxieties of core supporters who feel increasingly at risk when throwing their support behind a new leader. Conversely, the lack of visible power-sharing under Xi among China's powerful clans indicates a fault line that could open up into a chasm.

Under Xi, China has been inching back to the isolation that has characterised its history, from the time the Qin emperor built the Great Wall, as much to keep Chinese in as to keep invaders out, through Marco Polo's stay in the imperial compounds in the fourteenth century; to the Boxer Rebellion of 1900, when foreigners throughout the country were attacked as spiritual pollutants; the 1949 revolution, after which China broke relations with foreign countries and refused exit to most Chinese; and the Olympics period, when it was judged best to keep people from coming to see the Games. Under Xi, criticism from within and without has been controlled by the denial of visas to foreigners and exit permits to Chinese, banishing populations considered dissident from Han bastion cities along the eastern coast and using the social credit system to restrict the activities of people deemed to be unreliable due to debt. Foreigners are leaving China, and very few get back in. Investment flows are declining, as mutual hostility and mistrust rise between China and other nations.

CHAPTER FIVE

THE RETRACTION
THE FIFTH DECADE (2019–)

The fifth decade of China's opening began with the first known outbreak of coronavirus, or Covid-19, as it became known. The pandemic began at the Huanan Seafood Wholesale Market in Wuhan in November 2019. By the time the World Health Organization declared Covid-19 no longer a "global health emergency", nearly four years later, it had resulted in nearly 7 million confirmed deaths worldwide, making the virus one of the deadliest in history. China was one of several countries that underreported its cases, thus the count is likely much higher.

The Huanan Seafood Wholesale Market is geographically proximate to the Wuhan Institute of Virology, where researchers develop and study dangerous viruses, and the pandemic may have escaped from that lab through lax controls and human error – perhaps a tea lady or janitor smuggled out a lab animal and sold it in the wet market. But China is so constructed as to default to secrecy in the face of problems: no one wants to be blamed, since the government scapegoats individuals and applies draconian penalties. Keeping information out of circulation is the best way to blur the lines of responsibility. Every time there is an advance in understanding the origins and genetic makeup of the virus, China closes down the channel of information that made the advance public. As a consequence, foreign governments grow more suspicious, and conspiracy theories circulate about dastardly plots perpetrated by evil geniuses in Beijing.

As usual for events that make its leaders look bad, China's response to the pandemic got caught in a bureaucratic labyrinth of obfuscation, pursuit, and recrimination. A doctor in Wuhan who had tried to warn people about what was coming was muzzled by the government. Efforts by foreign countries, and probably by China's central government, to unravel what had happened met with stonewalling.

At the start, no one really knew how dangerous Covid-19 would be, and China overcompensated by locking down the whole country. The control methods used soon brought China back to the surveillance state of the 1980s and earlier. Since the pandemic, the restrictions have been relaxed, but the experience reminded the population that granular social controls are still available to the Party, whether or not they are in use.

The principal means of managing the pandemic was the isolation of potential infection carriers, partly through early detection but also by separating from the general population both close and second-degree contacts in quarantine facilities nationally. Cities built new facilities, and quarantine rooms were set aside for travellers in designated hotels. It became very hard to travel around China or even to get into office buildings and housing compounds without a pass.

Tight social control became routine, and many people suspected that the leadership welcomed this apparently unavoidable return to 1970s-style restraints. The lockdowns brought out of the woodwork a network of local people charged with keeping the order in their communities, and some of these people resorted to extreme measures, like walling people into their homes, electrifying fences, and refusing to let people leave their homes even for emergency medical care or after an earthquake. The central government blamed localities for poor management, but Chinese governance involves virtually no consequences for violations of individual rights but fearsome penalties for failing to carry out mandates from above. It was not surprising, then, to find people left to die in the street from ailments unrelated to Covid-19 or left at home without food and water, as long as the local case count didn't rise.

Soon, a phone app was invented to aid Covid-19 control, and the whole country had to rely on red and green codes to access buildings and public transportation. Along with local networks of retiree watchdogs, the app ratcheted up the levels of surveillance to which Chinese people are now accustomed.

Not so long ago, every village in the countryside and every street in the cities employed a few people to keep tabs on the rest. The Village and Street Committee representatives performed some useful tasks, like collecting bills, taking enrolments for social benefits, making sure food rations were delivered, and updating records on public health and literacy. But they also comprised a fearsome surveillance network.

The detailed information that these committees gathered and made available to the next level up in the government supported the political system by making a degree of totalitarian control possible. For example, local committees enabled purges in political campaigns by serving up 5 per cent of the population for punishment in response to Mao's claim that 5 per cent of people were undermining the revolution. The committee representatives contributed to fat dossiers on people, and the more information, the easier the search for dissident thought. The old personnel files were cradle-to-grave records of an individual's political reliability, used to determine privileges like Party membership, education and job opportunities, access to credit, eligibility for travel, and allocation of housing. They were secret and not available for review by the subject. People with some political authority could easily pursue personal grudges by inserting information into a personnel file that the target would never see. The lockdowns once again found Chinese people worried that enemies might wrongly designate them a Covid-19 risk.

SOCIAL CONTROL

At certain junctures in China's tech development history, various bureaucracies have tried to digitise the personnel file, with some of that bureaucratic energy coalescing around the plan to implement an individual credit score – Alibaba's version is probably the best known example of the kind and is called Sesame Credit. Social control by the Communist Party has always relied on two systems: blacklists and ranking. Blacklists, usually driven by quota, now focus on debtors, people involved in criminal cases, and people whose speech, actions, or ethnicity marks them as political risks. The second preferred tool of the Chinese nomenklatura is categorisation. Ranking of foreign organisations and individuals determines the level of surveillance applied to them. A key development goal of the Social Credit System is to automate the sorting of individuals into four levels: from A, for outstanding, to D, for serious lawbreaking record. Covid controls also made ample use of categorisation, sorting people into infection-risk categories and using copious personal information – such as national ID, address, and place of work – to do so.

The Chinese Communist Party fundamentally views itself as a ruler of populations rather than of people. That attitude was highly visible during the pandemic, when the health and welfare of individuals paled in importance compared with the ability of the government to claim victory over Covid-19 generally.

Covid control revived and relied on these old bureaucratic tactics and networks. Local authorities used online tools, and individuals relied on WeChat and websites to share information. Group purchasing networks developed spontaneously. But just as the old *dang'an* or personnel files were highly localised, there was no inter-regional or organisational data integration under the Zero Covid regime. China never developed an authoritative reporting system for infections and deaths. No one kept track of deaths that were due to Covid-19 but not from Covid-19 – for example, when hospitals refused to treat people with heart conditions or ruptured appendices. No one seems to know exactly what the control measures cost each level of government or how much was invested in quarantine facilities. The focus was on suppressing the case count and presenting a triumphantly Covid-free city to the central authorities, not on weighing the costs. In some ways, the lockdown campaigns demonstrated the degree to which local organisational incentives can trump big data.

During the pandemic, the whole country stayed home not for weeks but for years. The Chinese growth machine sputtered and nearly died, and everyone blamed the lockdowns. Economists, government officials, and normal people clung to the illusion that, if only people could get out of the house, the economy would resume its cheerful forward march.

But the pandemic masked a health problem afflicting the entire economy: the end of the real estate miracle. By the time of the pandemic, real estate – meaning land, construction, building materials, housing sales and mortgages, and everything else attached to property – accounted for about one-quarter of China's GDP. During the post-financial crisis investment mania, dependence on property had grown. That has meant multifaceted knock-on effects to the economy: weakening productivity, consumption growth that was dependent on capital gains from property, and low capital efficiency.

Expansionary economic times meant that the range of people who could aspire to social mobility, and even to wealth, grew rapidly. But throughout the years of investment fever, China neglected its social infrastructure. The central government's capital resources were directed at building visible, physical infrastructure, like roads and buildings, at the expense of investment in social services.

In the very first years of reform, Beijing and Shanghai built fancy, world-class airports, with scenic roads into the city centres connecting the airports with new five-star hotels that left foreign visitors spluttering with joy over the soaking tubs and crisp white duvets. Left unfunded were invisible targets, like public education, healthcare, retirement, and unemployment. The tendency to invest in eye-catching targets instead of less visible supports for human capital continue today; this is the curse of a bureaucratic system in which people are rewarded for immediate and tangible achievements.

During the property boom, China neglected the simple expenditures that would have prepared its poorer populations for the next stage of growth. Instead of providing rural children with eyeglasses, for example, or giving under-nourished people a multivitamin each day, governments poured money into constructing rural clinics that lacked staff with medical skills. Instead of requiring 12 years of education and making academic high school courses free, governments handed out subsidies to build unused training facilities. Given the imperative to push capital investment, China's educational curriculum, quality of healthcare, and efficiency of financial services all deteriorated as capital was concentrated in building physical facilities. The gains in health, education, and other types of well-being that were so prominent in the 1980s and 1990s fell off in the 2000s and may have gone backward. This foreshadows an intractable problem for the years ahead.

These issues represent a tremendous lost opportunity following a period of historically high investment and growth. They indicate the transitory nature of the China Dream and set the stage for China to fall back into reliance on cheap labour and low-value exports. This situation also demonstrates the likelihood that the impressive improvement in consumer lifestyles will stall. After all, Xi Jinping's definition of his core campaign theme, the China Dream, now speaks of a stronger nation and a "moderately prosperous" lifestyle for the Chinese masses, downshifting Deng Xiaoping's promise that someday everyone will be wealthy.

The whole Chinese economy has kited atop property speculation, and no official dared allow it to stop. The key value of property in China is optical: property values are a symbol of Chinese wealth, which must be seen to be growing as a source of legitimacy for the ruling party. Furthermore, highly valued property assets are dependable tender in the patronage system that supports the top-tier leaders, and they are one of the few places where high-net-worth families can park wealth with confidence that capital gains will be high and risks low. Finally, rising property values entrain construction, a sector of the economy dominated by state-owned companies that are key recipients of directed capital in the banking system and are important taxpayers, employers, and the fundamental constituents as well as agents of the political system.

All of this means that, for more than a decade following the financial crisis, the task for China's government was to freeze up the markets, trap value in property, and make sure that consumers felt rich on paper without actually being able to pull cash out of the market. That enabled banks to maintain the high book value of property that buoyed their loan books. Everyone understands that cratering property prices are what cause debt to be unsupportable. The property market became a stage on which governments and financial institutions played out a pantomime designed to present the appearance of a healthy commercial market.

After Evergrande, the pantomime became much harder to keep going.

NOT SO GRAND

The tsunami that began to wash over China's property sector in July 2021 was, in spite of its size, stealthy, as if an earthquake had lifted the earth's crust deep beneath the ocean floor that rippled up through millions of tons of water before forming a wave that hit shore. In summer 2021, to curb property speculation, Chinese regulators declared that banks should reduce lending for real estate.

Authorities had already been restricting loans to all but the most seemingly stable, publicly listed real estate companies. This prompted developers to make pre-sales two and three years before completing construction on new housing so that they could collect cash from buyers. Pre-sales have always been a big part of the Chinese market, but developers in the early 2020s, chasing cash flow, began selling as much as 90 per cent of inventory well before it had been built. As long as prices were steadily rising, buyers were happy to wait two years for apartments to be built, because they believed the value of their property would increase. But sales slowed, prices stopped rising, and buyers became more cautious. Local developers quietly abandoned construction projects. People halted their purchase plans. Banks slowed lending. Property prices weakened.

In August 2021, China's largest developer, Evergrande, warned of a cash crunch. The company soon missed a bond payment, and it formally defaulted on its debt in December. Evergrande confirmed over US$300 billion in debt, accumulated while the market still viewed property as a perpetual-motion machine.

It is hard to overstate the megalomanic vision represented by the Evergrande developments, visible in every city in China. The projects are visionary confections no less ambitious than the jungle palace of Mobutu Sese Seko or Angkor Wat in the forests of Cambodia. One drives through miles of jungle in Guangdong Province or over hills in Yunnan, and the entryway to the local Evergrande City complex appears like the gates of heaven in an old movie, only instead of Saint Peter, men in military-style berets guard the entrance. Cars are generally not permitted; one has to take a special golf cart, as if the complex were a giant movie studio and visitors were looking for the stars. Driving in, the dreary towns or gravel deserts surrounding the complex dissolve. Cherubs frolic in fountains, swans swim along canals, ducks waddle on landscaped grounds that generally host almost no people. The developments are lyrical and inspiring; one imagines a future when they will be filled with happy, wealthy families resting in the gazebos.

But their emptiness is a critical aid to the imagination. The lack of the practical facilities of life – proximity to places of business, adequate shopping, parking facilities, anything at all to do at night – in fact, the near Kabuki emptiness of the facilities acts as a blank screen on which a magical future can be projected. If prosperity gospel were stripped of its specifically religious content, its church would be Evergrande. By summer 2023, Evergrande had filed for bankruptcy protection in a New York court.

The 2021 default was only the beginning. The country seemed to be watching an iceberg melt in real time: when the top breaks off and falls into the warming ocean, that is the start of the crisis, not the end. Evergrande was just one among the developers that ran away with pre-sales money and abandoned construction on units that had already been paid for, and buyers were incensed. Pre-purchases basically halted. People with mortgages on abandoned projects refused to pay.

With sales shutting down, developers grew desperate. In Henan, a developer tried to entice buyers by asking them to pay in garlic, a local crop. Another developer advertised it would accept wheat. Soon, the government stepped in with cash and told cities they needed to complete the abandoned construction and developers they had to stop the discount deals: more than anything, policymakers feared a price collapse in property. Forget migrant workers and rural people: for a Chinese bureaucrat, hell hath no fury like a middle-class property owner scorned.

After the 2021 Evergrande bust, property began to deflate and developers no longer wanted to buy land. Sales of property dropped by about one-third in 2022, and land values sagged. That has had a doubly damning effect: local governments can no longer fetch a high price for transferring land-use rights, and the collateral value of land is in decline, meaning borrowers need more land to secure the same amount of debt. The end of real estate as the motor of development is sending local governments and the people they serve back into poverty.

The local government financing vehicle was the principal model used for the build-out of infrastructure under the stimulus plan. In addition to selling land, governments collateralise it for loans. As of 2021, publicly traded financing vehicle debt was around ¥40 trillion, 35 per cent of GDP, while many estimated that, including hidden debt, the real number is around ¥70 trillion.

High debt service, a poor share of tax revenues, and lower prices for land have meant localities can no longer provide many of the services for which they are responsible unless they borrow more money. The government companies mostly are supposed to be self-supporting, yet collectively, they lose money. But what do you do if the company operating a local subway system or hospital runs out of money? Since the consequences of failure would be very dire, cities have kept selling land, whatever the price, and finding new ways to borrow. Local governments long lived beyond their means and kept up only by selling more and more land. The local government financing vehicles became too big to fail.

To raise money, in the short term, cities find ways to fine companies and individuals, or they sell off assets like municipal parking lots, outdoor billboards and lightboxes, sometimes the right to operate a fleet of taxis or the local natural gas service. But in the longer term, none of this is enough. Next to go are pensions, health benefits, and even civil servants' wages. Bus drivers, doctors, nurses, and other public employees are online swapping information about waiting years to be paid back the wages they are owed. One local government-owned company caused public outrage when it was reported to have asked employees to take out consumer loans for their own wages: the company said it would eventually repay the loans.

Ultimately, the financing spiral had to end. In mid-2023 localities struggling under their burden of debt were curtailing bus services, cutting off heating, and closing schools and hospitals that didn't serve enough people. In some cases, employees of institutions that fail to pay salaries have complained to higher levels of government, but the responses tend to be either that the indebted institution is private, and so claims must be privately settled, or that corrupt officials stole money that should have gone to public institutions, and now the government is just broke. Either way, employees are out of luck.

Some homeowners are reverting to 1970s-level standards of living inside the complexes that once promised a new, luxurious life. Families paying mortgages on units that have been under construction for years at a time sometimes get fed up and move into the unfinished buildings even though the towers may have no glass on the windows, no water, no heating. The owners light fires to cook, use a local river to wash in, dig a toilet outside the building, or collect half-empty bottles of mineral water from local trash cans to use as drinking water.

The accumulation of debt is a familiar story among more developed nations. China's increasing reliance on debt was not in and of itself a bad thing. But what China lacks is a control valve, a connection between the power to deploy debt and responsibility to deploy it in a productive way. This lack of a control mechanism has meant that, even as debt grew visibly out of control, there was no corrective mechanism. Instead, all players in the system shared incentive to deploy more debt and to renew existing debt in order to fuel more investment. In a few short years, this syndrome brought China to the point where the country finds itself today: an apocalyptic landscape of empty towers, many unfinished, in every city and town and resort, on farmland, hillsides, even in the mountains.

The scope of this bizarre overinvestment is hard to grasp and impossible to measure with any precision. But there is no major city in China where it is not starkly visible in the ride from the airport to the city centre. The empty towers built in living urban locations are unaffordable to the new urbanised populations. And the empty towers built outside living urban locations are uninhabitable, with no jobs, no services, no way to live in them. There is no possible future for the empty cities across China other than to decay, for the cement and steel to revert to rust and rocks and gravel. But that will not be an easy process. Nor will the toll on the economy and the environment be low.

The wrenching dislocations of the property boom years, as people moved from villages where they knew everyone into anonymous high-rises, will inevitably show that the fabric of society has been badly frayed. Crime will be an inevitable result, alongside restless and unemployed youth.

SOCIAL BREAKDOWN

The Covid-19 lockdowns appear to have exacerbated China's social problems. As in the rest of the world, lockdowns created a sort of collective mental illness characterised by anger and suspicion – in no small part supported by the reality of China's harsh social controls. Conspiracy theories abounded. Public confidence in China's future faded.

The first of many city riots over pandemic controls came in Shanghai, which had suffered unforgiving lockdowns from March until mid-May 2022. Riots broke out over forced detentions and the separation of small children from their parents, lack of food, lack of medical access for any complaint other than Covid-19, lack of garbage removal, and much more. Members of the new Big White force of health workers with virtually limitless power to detain people in the community were filmed beating elderly people and ripping babies from their parents' arms.

At first, the riots did not spread. Few Chinese from less privileged areas make common cause with the people of Shanghai, who are seen as snooty and privileged. It was not until people in Shanghai protested in solidarity with Uyghurs in Urumqi, Xinjiang, following a fire on 25 November 2022 that the nation, at least briefly, rallied. The fire had broken out in a high-rise whose exits had been locked on account of Zero Covid policies. At least 10 people, including three children, died and at least nine more were severely injured – not coincidentally, the building residents were Muslim Uyghurs. It took three hours for rescue workers to respond. Urumqi residents went to protest at government buildings, and thousands of miles away, protesters went to Urumqi Road in Shanghai to offer the sort of implicit protest that is common in a political culture where criticising the Party can land you and your relatives in jail: dozens of cities erupted in sympathy with their own white paper or A4 protests – so named for the way protesters held up blank sheets of paper, knowing that slogans would get them in trouble. These protests were the biggest and most ideologically far-reaching since 1989. The protests catalysed sentiment that had been brewing for months.

What in another country might seem like minor perturbations in an otherwise placid political fabric in China can be ominous. So much political dissent occurs deep below the visible surface that elites and the press are often caught off guard. When Falun Gong protesters in 1999 surrounded the Zhongnanhai compound in Beijing, for example, an event that attracted a furious vengeance for more than two decades, very few people outside China had heard of this group. China's political arrangements remain hidden behind a screen and invisible to the outside world. The fact that no one knows how political decisions are made in China reveals just how antiquated the governing system is for this geographically huge, economically powerful, and culturally diverse nation.

The secrecy around government and the bare-fistedness of control measures reveal the measures political leaders are willing to take to hold onto power. China no longer attempts to persuade the West that it is a gentle giant that will grow into a cooperative partner in international governance. The internment camps in Xinjiang, the betrayal of Hong Kong, hostage diplomacy, intense focus on national security issues, truculent secrecy around Covid-19, and, most of all, economic weakness have shown the world that China's apparent desire to integrate into the global system of governance was temporary, provisional, and opportunistic rather than ideological. China is led by a Party that cares little for ideology and a lot for power. Much of the framework through which the West has understood China has actually been a shadow play, a drama acted out inside a lightbox while the real events are taking place in the darkened area outside the illusion.

PUTIN'S RUSSIA

Just as the world was getting on top of the pandemic, it was rocked by Russia's invasion of Ukraine in February 2022. The war brought into stark relief how pivotal China had become in international affairs. Potentially, China could tip world events.

That perceived role stands in contrast with the way in which China has conducted itself on the international stage. Despite its growth to economic prominence, China has appeared uninterested in integrating into global systems of governance. Consequently, China has not projected power in a way comparable to that of other great economies at various times, such as Greece, Ancient Rome, Germany, Russia, Japan, South Korea, Britain, or the United States. Given that the nation's historical memory is one of cycling regularly through volatile periods of union and fragmentation, China has seen its borders, its culture, and its people as threatened rather than enriched by contact with the outside. Although its economy for most of history has been the world's largest and most successful, China continues to view itself as the world's immobile centre, needing periodically to expand its borders to acquire needed resources but viewing trade as an inconvenience and investment in other nations much like missions of exploration to other planets, places you go well supplied, in constant contact with home, and returning as soon as possible.

This reflexive attitude of xenophobic suspicion coalesced when China cast its lot in with Russia following the invasion of Ukraine. The rally to Putin's side staked out China's reputation as an enemy of cosmopolitan liberalism. That was a turning point. The Party told its people that NATO threatened Russian sovereignty and that NATO somehow represents an extension of US power that is hostile to China. But that stance has not got much purchase. China in late 2022 and 2023 more or less dropped any ideological argument and fell back on its old strategy of fostering division in order to remain relevant itself.

Economically, China enjoys exploiting a position as middleman between a country that has been declared a pariah and other trading and political partners. China took prodigious advantage of US sanctions on Iran. During the US occupation of Iraq, China became that country's most important supplier of telecommunications equipment. China has long enjoyed a position as broker between the United States and "socialist little brother" North Korea, even though it is clear that China considers Kim Jong-Un's government an annoyance.

Opportunistically, immediately after the Russian invasion of Ukraine, China negotiated low prices for commodities from Russia and promptly bought lots of oil and gas. China pushed more renminbi at the Russian central bank, which raised the proportion of its foreign reserves held in renminbi. It ramped up rail container shipments to and from Russia.

In the end, China's potential gains from the conflict – mainly, cheap commodities – are minor, and what China stands to lose is major. Its uncomfortable alliance with a country that has become a flat-out dictatorship ruined plans that had been unfolding for two decades to make China influential in the international system of governance. International ambivalence over whether China is becoming a country ruled by law has ended.

THE TAIWAN THREAT

The Chinese Communist Party has long staked its legitimacy on the proposition that China has been humiliated by foreign powers, whether the territorial concessions that followed the

Opium Wars in the nineteenth century, Japan's occupation before and during World War II, the defence of Taiwan's independence by the Allied powers after World War II, or India's sanctuary extended to the Dalai Lama. According to this narrative, only the CCP is willing to fight to maintain China's territorial integrity: other rulers, such as the Qing dynasty and the Kuomintang, made treacherous deals with the enemy for their own convenience. Taking Hong Kong and Macao back from their colonial rulers, keeping Tibet and Xinjiang, and "regaining" Taiwan are therefore key to the Party's self-regard and claim to legitimacy. Since the time of Mao, Party leaders have been threatening Taiwan with seizure by force. Xi Jinping has revived some of this rhetoric. This time, the West has chosen not to ignore it.

There are reasons for Western fears. First, the Chinese military has modernised, vastly improved its communication systems, streamlined its command structures, and acquired a fearsome arsenal of weapons. In the 2020s, as opposed to the 1990s, China seems quite capable of conducting a military strike against Taiwan.

Second, the West worries about a "wag the dog" operation, as the Chinese economy continues to sag, and restive populations cease to be quieted by economic opportunity. Could Xi Jinping order an invasion just to boost his own legitimacy? Such things have happened in world history, and not infrequently.

Third, opportunity: the Ukraine invasion and a decline in US appetite for foreign wars may serve China an opportunity for invasion that could be lost in the future. Meanwhile, Taiwan is drawing further away from the mainland in political aspiration, and elections in Taiwan could increase this distance.

But there is reason to believe that the Ukraine invasion

served more as a cautionary tale for China than an object lesson about the extent of the possible. International reaction to Russia's invasion took China by surprise and may have acted as a warning of the unity of both public opinion and allied strategy, should China invade Taiwan. China's support is understandable: if China had not defended Russia in its invasion, it presumably could not expect Russia to defend Chinese aggression towards Taiwan. But China never imagined Europe would be so united so quickly. Specifically, China had not considered getting kicked out of the SWIFT (the Society for Worldwide Interbank Financial Telecommunication) international payments system: if that happened to China, it could devastate the economy. The freeze of Russian assets was also unprecedented and has ricocheted around interlinked contracts.

Conceivably, the Ukraine conflict may have prompted China to work a little harder to cut itself off from the West. Post-invasion, China's exports to the Belt and Road countries, which have received Chinese soft loans, have increased as exports to Western Europe and the United States have sagged, and Chinese authorities have said they want to move the economy away from pro-cyclical vulnerabilities.

China and Russia may nudge us into a world where dictatorships try to develop their own transportation networks to further insulate themselves from Western sanctions. Western shippers and freight consolidators have refused to pass through routes that touch Russia, and freight that goes by air is significantly hampered by airspace restrictions. When it comes to rail, China's rail and bridge crossings to Russia get bottlenecked easily. Those issues may prompt China and Russia to build new rail links. For some time, China has been trying to build a financial system that will be impermeable to Western sanctions. The efforts have not made much difference, because trading with the world requires openness and availability of currency. If, however, China were someday to shrink its network of trading partners to other dictatorships like Russia and North Korea, its dedicated financial system could become the principal one used for trade among those nations.

Economically as well as geopolitically, China is withdrawing from the informal pact that has governed its relationship with the world over the last 40 years. It is now evident that the experiment in Western capitalism that commenced in 1979 was a transitory phase, an acknowledgement that state capitalism could be deployed for a time in order to amass capital but that the new ways of doing things could also be discarded when no longer useful to the Party. Just as China opened up in 1979, so now is it closing.

China's emergence into the world economy has changed international political relationships, but not as a mirror to the postwar era. Instead of replacing the United States as the world's unipolar great power, China has altered the calculus that assumes, over the last century, that nations are fortresses and fully masters of their own political and economic fortunes. Now, people across the world feel bruised by 40 years of a brand of economic integration that has materially worsened their lives. Instead of blaming their own political leaders or their own mega multinational companies, they blame internationalisation itself. Relationships with China are a casualty: as much as China was welcomed as a Little Nation That Could, a puppy-dog-like aspirant to a seat at the international table, now China is being excoriated as a stealthy thief of the benefits of integration with none of the obligations.

Plutocracy has a different character in China than in the West. In the West, plutocrats actively promote policies that will increase their own wealth. Billionaires like Ray Dalio write books laying out their views, Elon Musk supports far-right causes via his internet platform, and Peter Thiel gives millions to preferred political candidates. In China, the wealthy class – princes of private equity like Eric X. Li and Neil Shen – loudly supports the political class, whatever policies those political figures may promote. Because China's political class relies on a small selectorate to keep it in power, there is no effort to influence public opinion other than, if needed, to keep people from protesting. But these are simply two flavours of the same brew.

Whether in China or the West, the fused political-economic class is very focused on unimpeded extraction of social resources. Plutocrats from Jack Ma to Elon Musk have endorsed a new political philosophy whose essence is the belief that the owners of vast wealth should deploy it unfettered by civil constraints, and somehow, the majority of the people will benefit. Akin to trickle-down economics, this concept has been irrefutably disproven by the broad public resentments described earlier. This philosophy looks new, burnished as it is with the idea of radical freedom, but it is really a recreation of the nineteenth-century idea that votes should be allocated by property, and that those without wealth are less competent to govern. In the US, the Supreme Court's decision in the Citizens United case authorised the right of the wealthy to buy legislators to do their bidding.

In the mid- to late-twentieth century, many in the West admired Soviet- and Chinese-style communism and hoped to emulate it. But after Stalin's and Mao's campaigns of murder became known, capitalism seemed a better bet for growth with less brutality. Among other things, capitalism featured the sanctity of private property and broad participation in resource deployment and protection of individual volition. People across the world didn't know what to make of China's change of policy, but command-control economics paired with authoritarian politics resulted in fast growth and so seemed to work.

Then came the financial crisis, and the world seemed to veer towards authoritarianism as a tool to crush the self-regarding plutocrats whose far-reaching plundering spread economic pain across much of the world. Since the period of investment-driven growth has ended, though, the West has grown disillusioned with the system of economic command and control that once seemed efficient at smashing bureaucratic resistance and creating prosperity for all.

At this writing, in 2023, authoritarianism appears to be on the wane. Admiration for Putin was checked by the *auto-da-fé* of Russia's Ukraine invasion. Brexit, propelled by nationalistic authoritarians, is driving the United Kingdom into international irrelevance. The American authoritarians have veered off into dark conspiracies that have no purchase with the majority of voters. And Xi's leadership in China looks increasingly hollow, as policies from Zero Covid to "property is for living" have been demonstrably flawed.

It is possible that the challenge China has posed to the world economy actually represents a temporary gap, a lag between structural change and the ability of political systems to understand and control that change. The period of the industrial revolution, after all, saw increasing disparities in wealth among populations in the US and Europe. Those disparities ultimately were reduced, as political systems addressed the relationships among business, labour, and government. Governments addressed monopoly power, strengthened unions, and built a thicket of social welfare protections and environmental and consumer protections to confine corporate greed. There are a few signs that the world is undertaking such an effort now, by reining in the internet companies, attacking monopolies, and looking at how to tax the international operations of multinational companies. But these are small and feeble steps.

The European experiment has demonstrated the frailty of attempts to preserve national sovereignty but gain advantages from unified currencies and immigration regimes. Especially after Brexit, the world remains largely arranged as a series of nation states, self-contained, sovereign, untouchable from the outside other than by violent encroachment. China, in the Party's zeal to remain unchallenged, is the most vocal supporter of that system.

That world order is antiquated and must be replaced with new international structures to manage money, facilitate travel and immigration, regulate actions that affect the natural environment, and address when and how countries must intervene to address humanitarian crises. The world's largest enterprises have aggregated more financial power and social power than most countries, yet their governance structures are the furthest thing from democratic, just as public responsibility is the lowest item on their list of priorities.

Bringing a new level of order to the currently chaotic world while preserving democratic choice is a tremendous challenge. That challenge was materially intensified as companies simply picked up and moved their operations to places like China, without regard for the citizenry in their countries of origin or impact on the Chinese masses.

Inequality of wealth, as documented by Thomas Piketty and Adam Tooze, is greater now than at any time over the last few centuries.

Isolationism is not the solution. Righting the balance will require an innovative re-globalisation model in which state players and major corporates recognise the existential threats of their established playbooks and reset their goals to encompass a fairer distribution of wealth globally, unwavering support for basic democratic and human rights practices, and otherwise use their power to create and maintain sustainable social and political stability on a global scale. Political systems must properly tax corporations and owners of wealth and deploy the revenue to right some of the imbalances generated over the last decades.

That is only a start. Anything less will prolong the unending chaos and disorder that now reaches every corner of our world and ultimately will serve no one well.

EPILOGUE

When my husband, Zhifang, and I left China for the first time, in 1988, getting him a US visa was not our most difficult challenge: that was reserved for the "exit permit" from Chinese authorities. To obtain this, we had to visit separate offices and wait in line – starting at five in the morning – to take a ticket that would allow us to be served after the offices opened, like at a bank. At each grim building, Zhifang officially turned in a different ration book – one office for the grain coupons, another for the monthly canister of gas and, last of all, his Chinese residence permit. He had to get stamps confirming his formal revocation of the privileges of Chinese citizenship before being allowed to leave. Such privileges, after all, do not apply to those presumptuous enough to leave the Middle Kingdom.

Over dynasties, Chinese leaders have viewed leaving China as an indulgence only the government can bestow, not as a right. In the Maoist era, the borders were almost entirely sealed, and thousands risked their lives to swim past sentries to Hong Kong or Macao or try to make it to Taiwan's outlying Kinmen Islands, just two kilometres from the mainland. Even in post-reform China, people have routinely been denied passports, and exit bans have long been in place for various ethnic minorities – since 2012 for Tibetans and 2015 for Uyghurs, for example, and an application for a passport to participate in the Muslim *hadj* could get the applicant put on a watch list. Chinese leaders view China as something akin to a family home and the Chinese people as the children of the household. With permission, children may leave the home to accomplish particular goals, such as education or work, but it is expected that they will return. The skeins of connection to Chinese society must not break, and the ability of China as a nation to control its people must not be abrogated.

After an exit interview by the police, Zhifang was finally permitted to leave. There was a moment when I stood on the Hong Kong side of the border, tending our pile of baby-blue luggage, my heart beating fast as a customs officer grilled Zhifang, but he made it through, and we got on the train to Central. It was like leaving a monk's cell and walking into a video arcade. The mainland was all grey and the navy blue of Mao suits, bicycle tyres swishing quietly along streets with tall, skinny trees in an orderly line on each side, skies the colour of a blister, canals filled with stagnant green water. Hong Kong – then still a British territory – was a riot of neon signs jostling for visibility, colour televisions in electronics stores standing "cheek by jowl" on shelves and all tuned to the same station, music blasting from boomboxes. On the mainland, world news came three weeks late, TV consisted of helmet-haired newscasters talking about the grain harvest in Henan or a state visit by the leader of an island nation no one could quite place. In Hong Kong, gangster films dominated, and the rogue cop or the renegade Chinese soldier would generally triumph over establishment figures.

Not only was Hong Kong a tumult of colour and activity, but it also felt free. No one reported to the police when you checked into a hotel. No one cared when you travelled in or out of the territory. No one followed foreigners around. In China, by contrast, we had to think about who was listening to our phone conversations, sifting through our trash, and reading our mail.

Over the decades, the two sides equalised, like hot and cold water mixing to make warm. Mainland China's streets burst into abundance. All the big cities opened electronics hypermarkets the size of football fields, with escalators carrying the shopper through level after level crammed with consumer goods. Shops began to compete for customers by placing huge speakers playing pop music at deafening volume on the sidewalks outside their stores. Hong Kong, meanwhile, slowly lost pride of place as a refuge from the tyrannical Chinese state. China started by kidnapping from the territory people it considered to be economic criminals, and eventually imposed its will on Hong Kong's legal system, which made it easy to arrest anyone in Hong Kong and spirit them to the mainland without cumbersome legal procedures.

✳

When Zhifang and I returned, in 1993, I was a lobbyist for US industry, and, with my employer, spent my time arguing that China should be granted Most Favoured Nation status and enter the international trading system as a peer. We argued that economic opening would bring political freedoms. In those years, everyone – Chinese and foreign – was filled with hope for democracy, reinforced by messages from the Chinese government. People like me met daily with Chinese officials who seemed disarmingly open and hopeful for China's boundless future.

The economic reforms prompted new freedoms that were thrillingly visible. China found that growth required a free job market that would allow people to move around for employment. It required a housing market so that companies would not bear the burden of building dormitories or apartment houses. Trade had to be de-monopolised. A private sector had to be permitted to grow.

All of this required a degree of liberty Chinese people had not experienced since before the Communists, if ever. Before the post-Maoist reforms, a manager at a factory or school or office held despotic, cradle-to-grave power to permit or deny weddings, funerals, job assignments, housing, or travel. A "leader" could even sentence employees to labour camps. Women had their menstrual cycles monitored and had to apply for permission to get pregnant. By the 1990s, Chinese people were free to travel, change jobs, marry and divorce, move around the country, and talk (privately) about politics without fear of retribution. It seemed that our theory of economic and personal freedom moving in lockstep was proving to be true.

But it turned out that many of the basic mechanisms of social control remained in place, however invisibly, even as the bonds that tied people to their native places and to their employers had loosened. It was as if the Chinese people were a team of horses and the economy a cart, and the Chinese Communist Party had decided to loosen the reins and let the horses run, but they never let go entirely. As long as the Party elite could maintain unchallenged control, with the wealth and social status that entails, China's political masters would let markets grow. Its own primacy was and remains the Party's core value, and it was always prepared to shut down China's capitalist experiment as soon as the people began to demand political competition.

The gauzy world that cossets foreigners (and wealthy Chinese) in China makes it easy to ignore a repressive political culture. Living in Beijing, we sent our children to foreigners-only schools with their own, internationally accredited curricula. We participated in a church congregation that was not open to Chinese passport holders – only those churches overseen by the atheists of the Party's Three-Self Patriotic Movement or the Christian Council may have Chinese congregants. Foreigners are left alone to worship, as long as they don't pollute the minds of Chinese. We could have as many children as we chose and move at will from city to city. We could complain openly about Chinese political figures and events without fear of retribution; we had little effect, after all, on public opinion.

In business, China's oppressive political culture was more palpable. But for me, as for the average Chinese person, most of the interference with business was tolerable, even exciting, as long as the economy was surging. In each business venture, my partners and I felt we were swashbuckling trailblazers, smarter than the big, slow multinational companies trying to curry favour with the Chinese government. Social changes were vast, and it all seemed worth the effort. Critically, everyone around me was getting rich.

When the hurricane stops, that's when you start to see the debris on the ground. Inevitably, the mania wound down, and making money was no longer easy. The political risks, the omnipresent corruption, the sheer grind of living in China started to chafe.

*

In 2014, we moved back to the US, following our children, who had settled there, and knowing that China no longer promised a brighter future. China has become much more repressive under Xi Jinping, and the tendency to wreak vengeance on those who dare to criticise anyone in power has only grown.

The threat of revenge for political slights was underscored in 2018, when China detained "the two Michaels", Canadian consultants, as bare leverage against Canada's house arrest of the Huawei executive Meng Wanzhou. Exit bans and detentions now represent a significant risk for foreigners visiting or residing in China.

The bans were only sparingly applied to foreign nationals, who have generally been viewed as rich but naive, unable to understand or participate in domestic politics. When the economy was humming and Chinese companies weighed heavily in portfolios, foreigners tended to ignore news about detentions, assuming that the detainee had broken a law. Now, with less economic growth to attract them, many are staying clear.

We returned as a family in 2019, just for a visit, and implicitly said goodbye to all the relatives. We promised another trip at the end of the year, but the Covid-19 lockdown gates dropped. Now, even with Covid-19 restrictions lifted, the possibility of being trapped on the mainland makes it unlikely that we will return before there is political change, and who knows when that could be. The system has already proven far more resilient than I expected.

In my personal as well as China's civic life, the chapter of giddy opening and exchange has now closed. For two and a half decades living in China and over 30 years travelling there, I and others like me felt like critical players in a crusade for a freer world. Now, humbled, we have come to realise that China is, as it always was, an ancient land with a political culture deeply resistant to change. China's breathless rise and its experiment in Western capitalism of the last four and a half decades were spurred on and shaped by the Party's survival agenda. The Party no longer needs the outside world. In fact, survival now dictates that it return to the isolation that has characterised so much of Chinese history.

ACKNOWLEDGEMENTS

Thanks to David, Chris, and Ken for forming all my ideas.

And thanks to Minh for everything else.

BIBLIOGRAPHY

Chan, Kam Wing. Buckingham, Will. 'Is China Abolishing the Hukou System?' *The China Quarterly*. 195 (2008).

Chase, Michael. Pollpeter, Kevin. Mulvenon, James. 'Shanghaied? The Economic and Political Implications of the Flow of Information Technology and Investment Across the Taiwan Strait'. California: Rand Publishing. 2004. http://www.rand.org/pubs/technical_reports/2005/RAND_TR133.pdf.

Deloitte. 'The Emergence of China: New Frontiers in Outbound M&A'. November 2009.

Du Yuhong. Sun Zhijun. 'Research on Compulsory Education Financing in China (*Zhongguo Yiqwu Jiaoyu Caizheng Yanjiu*)'. Beijing: Beijing Normal University. 2009.

Fairbank, John King. *China: A New History*. Cambridge, MA: Harvard University Press. 1992.

Huang, Yasheng. *Capitalism with Chinese Characteristics: Entrepreneurship and the State*. Cambridge, UK: Cambridge University Press. 2008.

Lam, Willy Wo-Lap. 'Rectification Campaign to Boost Cadres with "Red DNA"'. *The China Brief.* XIII/14 (12 July 2013).

MacFarquhar, Roderick, ed. *The Politics of China: Sixty Years of the People's Republic of China.* New York: Cambridge University Press. 2011.

McGregor, James L. *No Ancient Wisdom, No Followers: The Challenges of Chinese Authoritarian Capitalism.* Westport, CT: Prospecta Press. 2012.

Miller, Tom. *China's Urban Billion: The Story Behind the Biggest Migration in Human History.* London: Zed Books. 2012.

Mulvenon, James. 'Soldiers of Fortune: The Rise and Fall of the Chinese Military-Business Complex: 1978–1999'. *BICC Paper.* 15/99 (1999).

Naughton, Barry. 'The Scramble to Maintain Growth'. *China Leadership Monitor.* 27 (January 2009).

Naughton, Barry J. *The Chinese Economy: Transitions and Growth.* Cambridge, MA: MIT Press. 2006.

Naughton, Barry J. Yang, Dali, eds. *Holding China Together: Diversity and National Integration in the Post-Deng Era.* Cambridge, UK: Cambridge University Press. 2004.

Ong, Lynette H. *Prosper or Perish: Credit and Fiscal Systems in Rural China.* Ithaca and London: Cornell University Press. 2012.

Ots, Thomas. 'The Silenced Body', in Thomas J. Csordas, ed. *Embodiment and Experience.* Cambridge, UK: Cambridge University Press. 1994.

Palmer, David A. 'Modernity and Millennialism in China: Qigong and the Birth of Falun Gong'. *Asian Anthropology.* 2 (September 2012).

Peters, Enrique D. 'Implications of China's Recent Economic Performance for Mexico'. *FES Briefing Paper.* July 2005.

http://library.fes.de/pdf-files/iez/global/50197.pdf.

Pettis, Michael. *Avoiding the Fall: China's Economic Restructuring*. Washington, DC: Carnegie Endowment for International Peace. 2013.

Prime, Penelope B. Park, Jong H. 'China's Foreign Trade and Investment Strategies: Implications for the Business Environment'. *Business Economics*. 32/4 (1997).

Rogoff, Kenneth. Reinhart, Carmen M. *This Time Is Different: Eight Centuries of Financial Folly*. Princeton: Princeton University Press. 2011.

Rosen, Daniel H. 'How China Is Eating Mexico's Lunch'. *The International Economy*. Spring 2003.

Rozelle, Scott. Hell, Natalie. *Invisible China: How the Urban-Rural Divide Threatens China's Rise*. Chicago: University of Chicago Press. 2022.

Sanderson, Henry. Forsythe, Michael. *China's Superbank*. Singapore: John Wiley & Sons. 2013.

Shih, Victor. *Factions and Finance in China: Elite Conflict and Inflation*. Cambridge, UK: Cambridge University Press. 2007.

Spence, Jonathan D. *The Search for Modern China*. New York: WW Norton & Co. 1990.

Stevenson-Yang, Anne. 'China Government Subsidies Survey'. EU Trade Office. 2007.

Tidrick, Gene. Chen Jiyuan. 'The Essence of the Industrial Reforms', in Gene Tidrick and Chen Jiyuan, eds. *China's Industrial Reform*. New York: Oxford University Press. 1987.

Tsai, Kellee S. *Capitalism Without Democracy: The Private Sector in Contemporary China*. New York: Cornell University Press. 2007.

US Department of State Bureau of Economic and Business

Affairs. 'China: 1994 Country Report on Economic Policy and Trade Practices'. 1994. http://dosfan.lib.uic.edu/ERC/economics/trade_reports/1994/China.html.

Walter, Carl. Howie, Fraser. *Red Capitalism: The Fragile Foundation of China's Extraordinary Rise*. Singapore: John Wiley & Sons. 2011.

Wang, Shaoguang. 'China's 1994 Fiscal Reform: An Initial Assessment'. *Asian Survey*. 37/9 (1997).

Whalley, John. Xin, Xian. 'China's FDI and Non-FDI Economies and the Sustainability of Future High Chinese Growth'. *NBER Working Paper* (12249). 2006. http://www.nber.org/papers/w12249.

Wittfogel, Karl A. *Oriental Despotism: A Comparative Study of Total Power*. New Haven, CT: Yale University Press. 1957.

Yang, Dali. 'Economic Transformation and State Rebuilding in China', in Barry J. Naughton and Dali Yang, eds. *Holding China Together: Diversity and National Integration in the Post-Deng Era*. Cambridge, UK: Cambridge University Press. 2004.

Zhang, Liang. Nathan, Andrew J. Link, Perry. Schell, Orville. *The Tiananmen Papers*. New York: Public Affairs. 2002.

INDEX